MW00636917

Whispers From the Heart

Listen To Your Gentle Guide Within

Compiled by

Kyra Schaefer

Whispers From The Heart

Listen To Your Gentle Guide Within

Copyright © 2021. All rights reserved. The author is responsible for their individual opinions expressed through their words. The author retains the copyright to this book. No part of this publication may be reproduced, distributed, or transmitted to any form or by any means, including photocopying, recording, or other electronic mechanical methods, without the prior written permission of the publisher.

As You Wish Publishing, LLC
Connect@asyouwishpublishing.com

ISBN-13: 978-1-951131-42-5

Library of Congress Control Number: 2021925570

Printed in the United States of America.

Nothing in this book or any affiliations with this book is a substitute for medical or psychological help. If you are needing help please seek it.

Table of Contents

Chapter

One

We Just Need to Listen
By Rollie Allaire

Rollie Allaire

Rollie Allaire is a Holistic Life & Wellness Coach whose Spirit name is Geegado Megwan Kwe, which means Talking Feather Woman.

Since 2001, Rollie has drawn on her extensive career background of clinical psychotherapy skills and – in recent years – combined that with Energy Work, Chakra work, Crystal Reiki, ThetaHealing, Akashic Record reading and clearings, meditation, Moon Medicine teachings, and looking at life through the Medicine Wheel in the form of Life & Wellness Coaching and Facilitating.

She helps women with anxiety by giving them the ability to soulfully master their emotions, connect to their true power and learn to feel better in order to take massive action in their life so that they gain confidence, feel self-assured, strong, happy, and surround themselves with a supportive, connected community when they feel most isolated.

Rollie creates safe spaces both virtually and in-person for women to experience deep, life-changing transformations and healing. And she strongly believes that each person has the ability to heal themselves. Her job is to bridge the gap between the client and the methods that best suit their process. No matter what our experience in life, we can change our lives by taking action and not staying stuck. By helping ourselves, we help others who are struggling with similar experiences. No one comes through this world without struggle, but it's how we move through those struggles that get us to the other side.

She also owns Bridging the Gap Wellness Center in Haileybury, Ontario, where she works with other practitioners who provide their services within their small Northeastern Ontario community. She is a proud and loving mother of two adult boys, a wife, and a daughter. You can find Rollie at her website www.rollieallaire.ca.

We Just Need to Listen
By Rollie Allaire

I talk about using your intuition a lot. In fact, years ago, when I was teaching the "babysitting course" to the 11-12 years, I always mentioned listening to your gut feeling, if you thought someone was "creeping you out," even if that wasn't happening to someone else, to listen to it.

What is intuition? It's the ability to understand or know something right away without the need for conscious reasoning. It's also referred to as second sight or extrasensory perception (ESP).

Intuition comes to us in many different forms, but one thing for sure is that we ALL have an intuitive sense. We may not tap into it as we should, but it happens. Sometimes it's referred to as that 6th sense.

There are many tools that you can use to tap into that intuitive state. For example, you can use art as a medium to create something that simply allows you to "feel" or "interpret" a message, a thought, a feeling. You can use things such as oracle and tarot cards or pendulums. These are tools to help support your intuition.

For several years, my father has been ill. Due to many different circumstances, my father didn't believe in God or any other higher power. About 5 years before he died, he started seeing "little bonhommes" that would be running around the room. I believed they were spirits or beings that were there to support him. I met with a Medium who, without knowing he was ill, indicated that she knew he was ill and that he was getting "visitors." She said that at the time, they were far away. As he became more ready to die, they would get closer. That explained the "little bonhommes."

Over the last couple of years, before he died, he would have a "lady" that would interfere with him as he was trying to walk to the washroom. We would have discussions about who he thought she might be. We never did get a consensus. When he started palliative care, she would come into the living room, where she would sit and watch him. He didn't recognize her, but he felt comfortable around her. This was reassuring, given that he really struggled with the afterlife.

We were able to have a lot of conversations about this. It was increasingly more important to him as he knew his time was drawing nearer. It was also very comforting to me. My intuition told me that it was a combination of Spirits that would come and support him. The "playful" one in the kitchen who would interfere with him walking past was his mom. How do I know it was his mom? Because she would be the one who "teased" him. She was always very protective of him, even through his addiction. She shared with me years ago that the connection she had with my dad was very strong. He was always the protector. When my grandfather was injured, he was the one who would help her cook, clean, and do laundry. Even through his addiction, he was always a caregiver.

The one who would come and sit with him, I believe, was his aunt. They had a very close connection. She was the youngest of my grandmother's siblings. She was closer to my dad's age, and they spent a lot of time together. I believe that's who came and brought him comfort.

Do I know any of that was true? Yes, I do because my instincts tell me that. I've worked in mental health and addictions for more than 20 years. During that time, I would often "just know things" that I couldn't explain. This was very obvious when I had a very inquisitive student who would wonder how I knew certain things with my clients. There wasn't anything that I could put my finger on. I just knew.

For example, I had a client who was struggling with work, family, and life in general. She wasn't able to put any words or have any ideas of what was going on in her life. I kept insisting that she was grieving, but no one recently had died. She didn't lose her job, nor did she lose a relationship. As we continued to talk each week to figure out what was going on, I couldn't shake the feeling that she needed to work through grief. Finally, after about 6 weeks, she came in and said, "I think I know who I'm grieving."

Several years ago, she got pregnant. She and her husband had decided that they were not going to have any more children. And unfortunately, she ended up getting pregnant. She and her husband decided together that they would have the pregnancy terminated. She was okay with her decision then, as she still was. However, she felt like part of her was missing. We came up with a plan where she and her family (her children and husband) would have a private service to

6

honour their lost child. Together as a family, they named the unborn child. They had some memorial items and that they would honour that spirit. This provided her with the closure that she needed to eliminate the feelings of loss that she was unable to put her finger on. I saw her years later, and things were still going really well for her.

How did I know? I just knew.

I've had many of those scenarios with my clients that I simply couldn't explain. I often knew when they were lying or avoiding without them being direct. I didn't know at the time that I had this spiritual connection as I had grown up Catholic, and these types of things were not accepted by the Church.

What I didn't know growing up was that I was of aboriginal descent. We have many of our extended family members that, to this day, still deny our heritage. When I was about 10, my great-grandfather was not well. He just lived down the road from us, and we spent a lot of time with him. As he became older and getting close to dying, he often said, "We are not Indian," in French. In the 80's being "Indian" was a derogatory term for aboriginal or First Nations people. Even now, it's still not revered to be a positive thing. There is still a lot of prejudice against them.

At the time, I didn't understand it, but as I got older and learned about the treatment of aboriginal peoples, I understood why he would say this. Many of his extended family members who admitted to being of aboriginal descent were taken from their families. Reminding everyone that we were not Indian allowed us to be protected. Because of this, I was not able to learn my culture. In fact, it wasn't until I was in my mid to late thirties that I learned of our history. Before I even learned anything about it, I went to a function where it was lead by the drum. When the drum started beating, I was overwhelmed with emotion, and at the time, I didn't understand it. The Grandmother who was leading the Circle came to me and said, you have "Native Blood" coursing through your veins. That is why you feel it so deeply. I didn't know what she meant by that, but it stuck with me. When I started researching our ancestry, that is when I truly understood her message.

I am not someone who "sees" things. Even when I say, "I saw something," it's not really a vision with my eyes. It's a "sense" that I feel. I feel colour. I feel beings around me. I feel someone else's energy. My mom, on the other hand, actually sees things. If I am facilitating a circle, I will feel the anxiety sitting in my chest, but I know when it's not mine. Or I will feel a chill when a spirit walks into the room.

I don't ever believe that these spirits are negative or are ever here to harm me or anyone else around me. They are simply here, like the ones who came to support my dad. If someone says they have a spirit that feels negative around them, I believe they have been trying to get the person's attention to no avail, and they resort to doing something to get their attention. When the person acknowledges them, even if it's to ask them to leave, that energy leaves with them.

It's so fascinating that these messages come to us. As adults, we often don't see or hear these messages. My eldest son was 2 years old when his grandfather passed away. We all gathered back to the farmhouse after he had died. My son asked why everyone was crying. I told him that we were sad because grampa had died and wasn't with us anymore. He looked at me and said, "Yes, he's here. He is sitting on the corner on top of the freezer."

Children have this capacity to see and hear things that many of us lose the ability to be able to do. My youngest son had two imaginary friends. I believe that they were spirits that were around to support him. He would have full-fledged conversations with them. Some may think all of these things that I have shared are crazy, but it really is something that I strongly believe. When I've listened to my intuition, it has never steered me wrong. When I haven't listened, I've always had that hindsight that reminds me that I should have listened.

A prime example of that was when we were supposed to travel. We were preparing to go, and something said, "turn around." Initially, I ignored it, and we decided to still go ahead anyway. We then heard that someone we knew was in a fatal car accident. Based on the location of the accident, we would have been there or just coming up to the accident. Now I definitely listen to those little whispers.

Another example of children having this inner knowing that we don't listen to is the day my father died. Several things happened on that day that were completely unexplainable. My dad had this morbid sense of humour when it came to his death. So much so that it made some of my sisters uncomfortable. Where others, like myself, understood that it was his way of coping with his mortality over the five years that he spent "cheating death," as he would say. A few days before he died, I came across this couple who were signing "old country" songs. Songs that my parents would listen to when I was growing up. Then they started singing this song, "Hit the road Jack, and don't you come back no more no more no more no more." And I had thought to myself, "Well, that would be quite the theme song for my dad." I didn't give it another thought until the day that he died. My great-nephew came with my nephew to say goodbye. He's only 5 years old. My dad asked him to sing a song, and what does he sing, but "Hit the road Jack, and don't you come back no more no more no more no more." I wasn't in the room when he sang it, but my nephew told me about it. I laughed so hard.

Another instance that day was when we were all gathered around my dad as he was dying. My great-nephew stood with his parents. He was quietly saying things that his parents could hear, but we couldn't. Just as my dad died, my great-nephew said, "Pepere is gone now," audible for all of us to hear. And then said, "He's dead now." I looked up at the doctor, who gave me a little nod to acknowledge this. He was 100% right at that exact moment. My intuition says that he saw his spirit leave his body. I looked up and said, "You are right! He is dead now." It was truly beautiful.

I want to leave you with one more instance of that sad but beautiful day. My parents used to have a pair of doves that would be in the yard. A second pair of doves started coming around. Both sets of doves simply disappeared and hadn't been around for years. A few moments after my dad died, I went outside to the front of the house. I was talking to the doctor, and I happened to look back at the house, and there was a dove sitting on the wire above the house. I acknowledged the bird by saying, "Hello, little buddy. It's been a long time since we've seen you." I then started to cry because that was a message from my dad from beyond to let me know that he was there and that he was okay. No one had seen the dove the rest of the day. Nor has my mom seen it since I saw it that day.

We get messages all the time, and we simply just need to listen. And when we listen, we get remarkable messages. And when I acknowledge that, it's amazing how some things have just come to me. I was in my early 20's. I had gone home for lunch. We were only home because I insisted we needed to pick up a few groceries during my lunch hour. We were just putting the groceries away when the phone rang. As I walked up to the phone, I had said to my boyfriend, "My grandfather just died." I answered the phone, and it was my dad. His father had just died. I dismissed what had happened for a long time. It was just a "coincidence," is what I thought, but really it wasn't.

Someone asked me, "How do you know which spirit is around you that day?" And I believe that the person who has died that you think about at that moment is the spirit who is surrounding you. If I see a feather or notice a dime, whoever came to mind at that exact moment is that spirit who came to bring you a message. For example, I get a nudge that I need to do something (it's that inner knowing), and I see the message. It could be a bird or an animal. And then my uncle Mike comes to mind. Then for me, uncle Mike is there to support me at that moment, and what is the message? If it was an animal, then I will go a look up what that spirit animal has to say. And that's usually the message that I receive.

Sometimes these messages come to us in our dreams. I often have clients who receive messages from beyond. It could be perpetuating something that we are feeling anxious about. Or it could be something that hasn't yet happened. We simply need to pay attention to what is around us at the time.

For me, I know I'm on track when I have these "butterflies" in my solar plexus (the center point right under my ribcage), the hair will stand up in the back of my neck, I will get a chill up my spine, or I will get goosebumps.

The signs are all around. All we have to do is listen.

Chapter

Two

Mom's Heart In Hand
By Aileen Balizado

Aileen Balizado

Aileen Balizado, MA, holds a master's degree in Clinical Psychology and Organizational Development from Antioch University Los Angeles. She holds a bachelor's degree in Journalism/Public Relations from Northern Arizona University. She lives in Tempe, Arizona, and is the Founder of Lightworkers Connect: A Respite Resource Community.

Thank you to my best friend and editor, Lori Moerbitz, my "nonbiological sister" who I met at Northern Arizona University and Alpha Delta Pi Sorority. I am the Godmother to her daughter Erin. Aleysha and Rachel, my purple heart warrior sisters, with no questions asked, would be there for me. For more than 30 years, I have remained in contact with my Beacon faith-sharing sisters from Saint Monica's: Erin, [Tegan] Elizabeth, Natalie, Carla, Carleen, Bella, Annie and Geo.

To my Big Sky Meditation Community, my true Prayer Posse, and Earth Mothers: Dr. Catharine, Siv, Sheila, Dianne, Dr. Patti, Kimberly and Suzanne. I am supported by St. Monica Catholic Community in Santa Monica, California. This wonderful technology allows me to feel that I belong to my home parish. Mike "MC," Douglas "Papi," and Joseph S. You are my brothers of faith, and I am grateful for our friendship and your loving, prayerful support during this time in life.

My California sisters who relocated to Arizona, Thelma, Sue and Beverly, so many experiences of the ups and downs of life from funerals to weddings and even building a new home. Thank you all for loving me and supporting me through life and through death.

To my Goddess healers of Nuuaria, Maya and Lori. You continue to help me examine life and heal. As You Wish Publishing Kyra and Todd, thank you for having the platform to express my journey in the hopes that someone may be moved, touched or inspired. I am so blessed.

Email: aileenbaliz.lightworkersconnect@gmail.com.

Mom's Heart In Hand
By Aileen Balizado

T he world learned a beautiful heart and spirit left this earthly plane this past summer. My mother, Aurora De Vera Balizado, 83, passed away on June 27, 2021, in Scottsdale, Arizona. She was born in San Fernando Camarines del Sur, Republic of the Philippines, to Fausto and Felisa De Vera.

Aurora was married to the love of her life, Dr. Alfredo Balizado, for 40 years. They were blessed with five children: Arleigh, Mary Ann [Larry], Alfred, Aurora [Sean] and Aileen; and nine grandchildren: Rebecca [Alden], James, Sarah, John, Catherine, Alexander [Jessica], Evan, Michael and Joseph.

Growing up in a large, close-knit family from Naga City, Philippines, Aurora's childhood was filled with music and hearty laughter. Aurora was the fourth of twelve children: Angela Pinlac (deceased), [Adolfo]; Ernesto De Vera (deceased), [Matilda]; Gloria Concepcion (deceased), [Jesus (deceased)]; Nora Timpauer [Alberto]; Arturo De Vera [Maria Pilar]; Jesusa LaRosa [James]; Fausto, Jr. De Vera [Catherine]; Romulo De Vera [Amalia]; Manuel De Vera [Nerissa]; Maria Teresa De Vera [Jose Villaneueva]; Danny De Vera [Lourdes].

Aurora attended Zamboanga Hospital School of Nursing, where she graduated as a registered nurse in May 1959. She met Alfredo while working at the Infante Clinic in Isabela de Basilan.

Alfredo and Aurora were married on January 1, 1960. They operated a successful medical clinic in Lamitan, Philippines, until 1970. Ever the devoted parents, Alfredo and Aurora decided to move their family to the United States to seek a better life for their children.

Upon immigrating to the United States, Alfredo, Aurora, and their five children settled in Tempe, Arizona, where they soon established ties to their new home. Alfredo and Aurora were active members in the Arizona Philippine Physicians Association and the Lions Club, where they volunteered many of their hours serving others. Aurora was a devout Roman Catholic and an active member of the Mount Carmel Catholic Community. She loved attending daily Mass, praying the rosary, and providing support to all.

When she was not doting on her children and grandchildren, Aurora enjoyed writing poetry, playing mahjong, and even learned how to play the piano at the age of 80. Her piano rendition of "Happy Birthday" will be greatly missed! Aurora was an avid sports fan who enjoyed watching her beloved Phoenix Suns, win or lose.

Aurora will live on in the hearts and memories of all who had the privilege of meeting her. She will always be remembered as a strong Catholic woman who lived her faith. She was a dedicated mother and grandmother (Lola) who was devoted to her family. She treated everyone with kindness and generosity. Above all, Aurora, our mother, was a beautiful Child of God.

Dear Momma,

When you left us, your legacy was a fighting spirit and passion for life. I vividly recall the countless times we were together, hand in hand. You had an inimitable way of making yourself presentable, with your hair perfectly styled and nails manicured. This photo grid is my homage to you and our deep love. We will always be connected. In remembrance, I wear the earrings that you loved so much.

What a fashionista you were. We got you a vintage Channel purse and a pair of Channel glasses. At times, I can still smell your perfume, and it brings your memory back. Your love of butterflies and roses and your belief in Angels and God were inspiring. What a blessing to those who loved you to have these reminders of your grace.

We shared so many memories. You taught me to always look your best, and we had many "Mommy and Me Mani Pedis" and hair-do experiences. We held hands to take the "after" beauty salon pictures as you loved taking selfies. We've had so many bonding moments like these, and I ask myself how you did that, making each one of us feel so special, like we were your favorite child and only best friend.

I used to get annoyed when you picked the same color nail polish as me. My brothers and sisters would remind me that I should feel flattered. I would drive you to your Filipino hairstylist to have a great experience speaking in your native language. It was fun to watch you chat about people you knew, even though I didn't understand every word. It didn't matter as long as you had a good time.

I often think of your love for celebrating holidays and birthdays. We all have wonderful memories of your big 80th birthday celebration and loved the photo montage that your grandson Evan put together to music. All five kids said a reflection, and I shared a prayer of the 23rd Psalm that you and Daddy taught us because all that was said about you would have been repetitive. Your love of God and daily prayer was something you held highly, and every day watched the rosary and the Chaplet of Divine Mercy on EWTN.

When you were sick and in the hospital, we prayed for your healing, but when the doctor told us it was time for compassion care, we prayed for your comfort and peaceful transition. That was a testament to your love of life and the values you taught us. Even though you lost your voice, when we could communicate, your concerns were about paying the bills on time and making sure you had your medications. As an RN, you knew that when you were taken off your medications, there was to be no more struggle, and you could let go of the fight. And then you were gone, leaving all of us with a hole in our hearts that will never be filled. Only your spirit is left there. I know that everyone who met you loved you. After your death, I went to visit the pharmacy, and they had heard the sad news of your passing from my brother. The pharmacist let me know you were there the month before and had dropped by to just say hello because her children had already picked up her prescriptions. So friendly of you, Momma, our social butterfly.

I am so grateful for this time to write a collaborative book that allows me this cathartic experience to help process the grief. It's such a painful and profound journey. Some of the hardest times are when I forget you are gone, and I wait for you to come home from dialysis to ask you, "how should we prepare dinner?"

I reminisce about how you would watch me from the kitchen counter and ask me what I was cooking and tell me how good it smelled. In your stronger days, I would be your prep chef, but you would put it all together. Every Filipina cook has their own take on how to flavor their adobo or pancit, and yours was the best. I watched you fiercely but never could duplicate your actions because you would cook by sight and never measured. Your food was so delicious, better than any restaurant in the world.

The grief process has been extremely challenging for me. However, I am supported by many resources such as St. Monica Church through the Internet and Zoom. This wonderful technology allows me to feel that I belong to my home parish. Thank you, Christine Gerety. Thank you to my healers, grief therapists and wellness coaches. Thank you to my friends who are in the unfortunate "dead parent club" or "adult orphans." Thank you to my then Manager, Tammy Paul and HR Manager Kelly Morse who had the insight and compassion to support me to take time out to tend to my new life as a retired caregiver and daughter without parents. I have to thank my team for reaching out and sending love when I was in my pain bubble. All the communication, cards, flowers, gifts, prayers, and thoughts were so incredibly appreciated.

Momma, I still talk to you in my heart and on hard days out loud, Momma and Daddy. I visit your resting place reunited in heaven. The photo collage I chose over a current picture depicts the many times we held hands, Momma. The post-manicure pictures, the childhood photo when you held my hand, the Mayo Clinic which allowed us to visit you while suited up in the Covid unit, showing the blessing of my holding your hand when you took your last breath. I am so grateful my brother-in-law Sean held your other hand, and you were not alone, as I was not alone in this last precious moment. It was deeply sacred.

The Nine Day Novena and Litany of Faithful Departed souls online was well attended by guests participating in prayer with our family from across the world, such as Africa, Arizona, California, Canada, Delaware, Guam, Hawaii, Philippines, the United Kingdom and Virginia.

At your wake, we held hands again as you had your rosary wrapped in your prayerful state. We all had written cards and letters for you. The heart-shaped rose quartz crystal accompanies a letter that I placed with you in your casket.

Planning a funeral over the Fourth of July weekend during Covid and blocked borders was a challenge in and of itself. During the monsoon season, the roof leaked and flooded my previous home office, and a pipe leaked in Momma's room. I left my job for a six-week period of bereavement leave and tended to the industrial fans, demolition crew, construction crew, insurance agents, and all the people involved, knowing that contractors have their own time frame. I could swear Momma had this happen on purpose so that it forced me to engage with people. I wanted to die with you, Momma, and it forced me to live my life when all

I wanted to do was curl up in a ball and puddle of sorrowful tears.

The grief comes in waves, from howling cries to whimpers or just leaky eyes. Your presence is missed. So many well-intentioned people had the most inappropriate comments. Some communications were so ridiculous, with this lack of grace added to the burden and the much too-little-too-late apologies for premature announcements of my mother's death and sharing of misinformation. For instance, she was never intubated. In this new anger stage of my grief, I want to say to people, shame on you for your lack of compassion, and gossiping, and spreading misinformation. Anger is a natural part of the grief process. That irresponsible communication caused much confusion and despair in the community that loved her.

In the business of death, a lot of people had repeated requests for an original copy of the death certificate, and I felt no grace and compassion in them. Jesus said, "Forgive them for they know not what they do," or saying for that matter. It's not ok. I had my mother's home phone disconnected, so I don't have to explain to one more charity that she is still dead and will not be able to pay your donation or pay that bill, and then let fly an expletive or two. No, our house is not for sale, and no, you cannot have a house tour. Please respect that we are grieving. Thank you. To these seemingly thoughtless people, it's not how she died; it's how she lived. So there I said my piece.

My mother was the best mother in the world. She was very forgiving, faithful, and loving to many. Momma Aurora and Papa Alfredo were smart, well-educated, strong, kind-hearted, faith-filled parents and their descendants are their legacies. These are big shoes to fill, but I, my siblings and their children are up for it.

Recently, my friend Tegan passed away unexpectedly, and I felt that she was so very lucky not to have the responsibility of living on this earth anymore. May she rest in peace. A counselor told me that was depression thinking when death sounded better than living. My friend Sole told me to be gentle with myself as I have been through so much. I would talk with her for hours of my anguish and pain, and she listened to me vent with such understanding.

I remembered that someone once wrote, "A cut finger goes numb before it bleeds, it bleeds before it hurts, it hurts until it begins to heal, it forms a scab and itches until finally a scar is left where there was once a wound." It's an apt description of grief.

"Grief over the death of a loved one is the deepest wound we will ever have. Like a cut finger, it will go through many stages before it leaves a scar. Our grief may manifest itself in anger, bargaining with God in disbelief, depression, and many other emotions. These feelings may repeatedly occur without any warning or order, but the thing to remember is that they're normal. They are as natural as sleeping when we are tired, eating when we are hungry or sneezing when our nose itches. They are nature's way and God's way of healing a broken heart. Grief provides peace and growth, but we are the ones that have to seek that treasure and be willing to sacrifice anything to possess it," Mauryeen O'Brien, The New Day Journal. A Journey of Grief and Healing.

For my friends, I have joined the unfortunate association of adult orphans. For motherless daughters, I hear you, see you and feel for you. In the end, we are all on the same ocean but on different vessels. The death of my mother is the deepest heartache and heartbreak I have ever experienced. When my Daddy died, it was very difficult, but when Momma died, both parents were now gone from this earth. I was lost, so incredibly sad, and in shock. My bereavement group understands; the team of support from Christine, Daniel, Steve and Catherine is so incredibly compassionate. The participants cry, pray, and release distressing experiences. Our gaping wounds are heard and felt, and we move and touch one another with our stories of our dearly departed loved ones from infancy to the elderly, no age group untouched. This is my village, my family and my support community.

Whenever I see butterflies, I will think of you. I whispered in your ear, "Momma, send me a sign that you are at peace." When we returned home from the hospital, my brother, who was sorting through the mail, handed me this wallet and asked if I wanted it, it was in her things. It had butterflies and roses. I heard coincidence is God's way of remaining anonymous. This message was for me.

Thank you, Momma and Daddy, for creating our lives. We are your proud children and so very proud of our heritage. Your legacy of service, compassion and light live on through us, and we will continue to share our stories so that you will live on in future generations.

Don't go it alone. Find your village of healers, wellness coaches, trusted friends, family and for the love of God. I am so grateful and blessed to have been given this voice to share my light in the hope that it helps others.

I dedicate this book to my family: my siblings Arleigh, Mary Ann, Alfred and Aurora-Mom's namesake. We were all delivered by our father, who was a physician, and some of us were even born in the house. Our strong family bond started from birth. We joke that we have the same belly buttons because Daddy tied all of our umbilical cords the same way. There are no other children with the same combination of DNA on this earth. We planned and supported each other through the two funerals of our parents. Now we are adult orphans together. Thank you for being such good siblings to me. I can never express how grateful and blessed I am to be part of such a loving and supportive family. God has been very good to us to have such wonderful parents, and now it's our turn to live out their legacy of generosity, positivity and carry their light.

Chapter

Three

For Better, For Worse
By Rose Bourassa

Rose Bourassa

Rose Bourassa is a retired procurement specialist and international bestselling author. She is currently preparing for a second career as an evidential medium. She is a mother, grandmother, student, teacher, artist, and volunteer. She strives to learn something new every day to keep sharp.

Hopefully, something to help keep up with grandkids. Even when they have to dumb it down! You can reach Rose via email at Remnick@aol.com.

For Better, For Worse
By Rose Bourassa

A few years ago, a friend of mine was getting married. He made a statement that they would stay married as long as they were happy. I was taken aback by that statement.

Marriage seems to be on the list of disposable things in life. When I married in 1982, those vows were worth their weight in gold. *"For better, for worse, for richer, for poorer; in sickness and in health, to love and to cherish, till death do us part."*

I can't say marriage has been all peaches and cream. We've had our fair share of ups and downs, but we stuck it out. We worked it out as best we could. Then we lost our son in 2014. The death of a child is a game-changer in a marriage. You either make it through together, or you don't. I will admit there were times I was ready to say, "I'm done; I can't do this anymore." We were on different emotional playing fields. While I found outlets for my emotions, he hid his.

Someone once asked me why I didn't divorce him. "Because it's cheaper to keep him." My standard answer. There was too much at stake, too much to lose in a divorce. The only one who wins in a divorce is the attorney. But truthfully, I could not imagine my life without him in it.

When the world closed down for Covid, I was working through a most stressful time. My demanding job got more challenging. All the things we did before Covid took on new meaning and raised my stress level. While I worked, my husband took care of things like grocery shopping. He did all the running around, so on my days off, I could sit in a corner and stare blankly at the world—my two-day mental shutdown.

On Wednesdays, I worked from home. Last August, I started noticing a cough. The following week, the cough was worse. He had Covid. I was confident he had picked it up in his travels. We went to get tested, and the doctor noticed some crackling sounds in his lungs. He took an x-ray and discovered both lungs had pneumonia. He gave him meds and sent him home to follow up with his primary care doctor. The test was negative for Covid, but as pneumonia cleared, they found the reason for the cough. Lung cancer. Stage 4.

The oncologist laid things out for us. Two months if you do nothing, maybe 18 with chemo. No brainer, we were going to try chemo.

Chemo is not fun. He had a few bad days in the cycle in the first few rounds, but it put his cancer in check. They changed the drugs to a "maintenance" drug. Those rounds were "well-tolerated," to quote the doctor, but his cancer began to grow again. Again they changed the medications as per the "protocols" the oncologist told us. Who made up the protocols? Who decided on these drugs. These sent him into a tailspin. The side effects started the day after treatment and got worse and worse. At one point, he was so dehydrated I had to take him to the hospital for hydration treatment. When he came home that afternoon, he could barely walk. It was challenging to get him from the car to the bed. Three hours later, he was in the bathroom, on the floor, on his hands and knees, trying to get up. I attempted to help him up. My daughter's boyfriend was over, and he tried to help me get him up. We finally decided to call the fire department for help to get him up.

The firemen came, and when they saw him on the floor, they questioned what was wrong with him. They summoned the paramedics. We provided his medical history, and the medics discovered he was in A-Fib. His heart was beating at a very high rate. The ambulance came, and they rushed him to the hospital, where he stayed for several days. They released him to go home on our 39th wedding anniversary. Unbeknownst to Michael, I had planned a small gathering of friends and family to help us celebrate. With his illness, I didn't know if we would have another one. I had to cancel that party. Friends who were part of our wedding party all those years ago stopped by with a cake and ice cream anyway. The celebration was short but meaningful.

His next chemo round was only one drug and 80% strength. His doctor was trying to keep cancer controlled and reduce the side effects at the same time. That didn't work so well. After two rounds on the new cocktail, we were back in the hospital. As luck would have it, our regular hospital was closed to ambulance traffic, so they sent us to another facility. They checked him up one side and down the other and discovered diverticulitis and inflammation in the bowel. They needed to insert a tube to drain the infection. So much to deal with at one time.

It was overwhelming. He stayed for an entire week before being transferred back to our regular hospital and placed in the rehab unit in an attempt to get him up out of bed and walking again. While there, he decided he had had enough. "No more chemo. I'm done."

His was a very bold statement, one my daughter and I had discussed several times. We could not understand why he continued when it made him sick, knowing it would not change the outcome. The decision was his to make. We could not make it for him, but we did support it 100%. We also hoped that physical therapy would help him be mobile again, and he would have some time feeling well before things went downhill.

That hope faded away when he announced he had decided to come home on hospice care. We know about hospice care—in places other than in our home. We met with the hospice liaison at the hospital. Look up "overwhelmed" in the dictionary, and you will see my picture. The house needed to be reconfigured to accommodate a hospital bed, the wheelchair, the oxygen equipment. I was so not ready for this and had a total emotional breakdown. I was ill-prepared to deal with what was to come in a mere 72 hours. I thought I would have more time to prepare.

Like manna from Heaven, a friend appeared and redesigned my house and helped move furniture around. A few hours later, two more strong bodies arrived and moved the last two pieces. That was Thursday.

The hospice liaison had given me a list of caregiver agencies and said I should line up some help. Friday, I made a few calls. Talk about feeling clueless! I learned I had no idea what I would need for outside help until he came home.

Sunday, he returned home via ambulance. Then the challenge began. We had set up the hospital bed in the family room. I now had to share custody of the TV remote control. That was a huge issue. We don't always like to watch the same shows. Before hospice, he had converted our spare room into his "sick room." There he had a recliner and a tv all to himself. Now he is in the family room and wants control of the remote! Really? Here it was: another one of those messy marriage issues. Who controls the remote? Flip a coin?

Things were good in the beginning. I was into some exciting creative art projects outside on the patio, so I did not watch tv until after dinner. We eventually worked out a happy medium for tv, but if he fell asleep with the remote in hand, he would have a death grip on it. Once, I told my daughter I felt like I would have to bury him with it since it was so hard to pry loose from his hand. I wondered if the Incredible Hulk would even be able to get it away from him!

It took me 48 hours to figure out the exact type of outside home health care I needed. Having someone in my home doing nothing for 4 hours at a time was not what I needed. I needed help changing the adult diaper. I will never complain again about changing a baby's diaper! No matter how messy that baby diaper is, it is a walk in the park compared to trying to change a grown man who can't move too well. After two days of me rolling him back and forth trying to get the diaper and the mattress pad in the proper position, he insisted I hire outside help. He admitted this part of the job was not for me. It had been a long time since my high school nurses' aid training. I can still make that hospital corner on the sheets when making the bed. But adult diaper changing? Oh, heck no! I failed big time.

We had a visit from our social worker, and I mentioned my need for help on this matter. I could handle the meals and everything else he wanted. Hospice was sending in a lovely lady twice a week to bathe him. Thankfully that was already covered for me. The social worker handed me a flyer on a new service in town—exactly what I needed. I hired them the same day. We were both pretty happy now.

Then the decline started. Small things at first. Very gradual, but I could see it happening daily right before my eyes.

One morning, Michael did not wake up. He did not return my "good morning pop." The caregivers came and changed him a few times, all without comment. I called for our hospice nurse to come and assess him. She was on vacation, and they sent the backup nurse. Nice guy, but all business. After checking his vital signs and telling me all the numbers, he asked if I had lined up a mortuary yet. Then they lowered the boom. I was looking at 24-72 hours before he would change his address to Heaven. I must say I was taken back a lot on that statement. You always think you have more time until you don't.

That night, I decided to sleep in the recliner next to his bed. He hadn't spoken all day. I didn't even know if he was still in there or not. At 10pm, he asked for a popsicle. A grape popsicle. What? "They told me you are checking out, and you want a grape popsicle?" So I went to the freezer where we had a brand new box of cherry, orange, and grape. I opened every darn one looking for grape. *No grape!*

Holy crap! What the heck? No grape! I am suing the manufacturer for false advertising. My dying husband wants a grape popsicle, and there was not a single one in this brand new box. What kind of wife am I that I unknowingly buy a defective package only to learn I can not fulfill his possible last wish? He settled for cherry and was happy.

The following day he wanted oatmeal for breakfast. Here you are 12 hours into that 24-hour zone, and you want oatmeal. He ate a bite or two and went to sleep for the rest of the day. When he woke up, he wanted another grape popsicle that we did not have. We continued like this for the entire 72 hour period. When we hit hour 72, I was like, "What the…?" Guess only God knows when your time is up, and the nurse was not God!

A few days later, he asked for his wedding ring. We had taken it off at the hospital because his hands were so swollen. Now they were normal again, and he wanted his ring back on. As I placed it back on his finger, he said, "Gee, I must have gained some weight; it fits fine." Okay, pop, you can believe that if you like. I won't burst your bubble while trying not to cringe at how thin he had become.

The following day, the bath lady came. She had a way with him. A little flirt here, a little flirt there. Hearing this camaraderie, I asked him to hold up his hand. When she saw his wedding ring, she faked having hurt feelings. It was the cutest thing. She told him all about being dumped for that beautiful lady on the couch and why he had not told her sooner; he was married. How rude! It was lovely to see him smile.

The following Thursday, he was unresponsive again. The night before had been trying; traumatic. He called out a name at midnight that woke me up from a sound sleep. As I rushed out of the bedroom to get to him, I ran into the door. Surprisingly, it did not cut me down the middle, but it sure felt it did. When I got to him, he was talking randomly about stuff. He wanted to know where his friend was. His truck was in the driveway, but he didn't see him. "Where is my phone? I gotta text 911 and tell them I'm going. Where is my phone? I gotta make a call." After thirty minutes of this, I texted the friend and told him he should pay him a visit in the morning as he needed to see him. I finally figured out he was in pain, too. When asked if he was in pain, he instantly replied, "Yes. I'm a six." So I went to get the meds.

I continued to sit with him for the next two hours. I answered weird questions and kept explaining why he was not going to call anyone in the middle of the night. At one point, he told me there was a party going on and pointed to the ceiling. I asked who was there. He asked for his glasses. I never did find out who was at the party. I granted permission to attend if he so desired. Eventually, he had another round of pain meds and a pill to help with the anxiety he was experiencing and sharing with me. About 3:30am, he finally settled into a new peaceful sleep.

When we woke up Thursday, he did not. The bath lady appeared and began his bath with no words from him at all. Then she asked me if I had removed his wedding ring. It was not on his hand. My heart sank. Where could it be? I wondered if it somehow made its way to the trash during one of the bed changes. He's not talking, and the ring is lost. That's when I lost it. Holy heck! Today is trash day. I need to bring the trash cans back in so I could dumpster dive and find his ring. Luckily, it was found in the sheets and had never left the bed.

Nothing could stop the tears that came. I was overwhelmed at the thought of losing both my husband and his wedding ring. My wonderful bath lady came over, hugged me, and told me it was okay to cry whenever I needed to. Strong women cry, and that day, boy, did I need to cry! Before she left, I called my hospice nurse, asking her to come and access him as he was non-responsive again.

She came, she saw, she told us he was beginning to transition to the other side. I'd heard that story before, but this time it hurt worse to listen to it again. It seemed more genuine this time. There were no words from him the entire day. The next day, the maid of honor at our wedding came and spent the day with me. We prayed over him, knowing he heard us. Several other visitors came and went. That night, I caressed his face and told him how much I loved him. He opened his eyes and said, "I love you too." There were no sweeter words ever spoken. I told him I was sleeping on the chair next to his bed that night. He nodded yes in approval.

Our social worker checked in that week. As I told her the events of the week, she reminded me there was no greater expression of love than having him home with our daughter and me. All the tears I cried seeing him this way and my desire for him not to suffer anymore was just more love pouring out from my heart through my eyes.

Every night before I went to sleep, I would tell him I loved him, and if our son came and said, "Dad, it's time you came to be with me on the other side," he was free to go. His girls would be okay. Even though he was unresponsive, I could feel his heart whisper to mine, "I love you too."

We held fast to our marriage vows right up to till death did us part. I lost my husband, and my daughter lost her father in the early morning hours on August 15, 2021. Our hearts ache, and we will cry a million tears, but at long last, he is out of pain and at peace. Fly with the Angels, my love! Until we meet again....

In loving memory

Michael O Bourassa

11-26-1948 to 8-15-2021

Chapter

Four

Remember Who You Are
By Beth Eiglarsh

Beth Eiglarsh

Beth Eiglarsh, a self-proclaimed perpetual student, was born with a gift of compassion and sensitivity. After years of success in the travel and advertising industry, she founded her own company in 2003. The Julia Taylor Collection, lovingly named after her daughter, specializes in custom-designed and hand-crystallized upscale gifts. Her work was featured all over the US and Caribbean and was included in the Oscar and Grammy celebrity gift baskets. A global partnership with Bacardi placed her VIP gifts in Dubai, Abu Dhabi, France, Norway, Poland, Australia, Thailand, and the UK.

In 2009, Beth was drowning in workaholism and found herself operating from a place of chaos, fueled by fear. After hitting her rock bottom, followed by intense introspective work, Beth was gifted the opportunity to realign with her essence, purpose, and mission. Today she is a Certified NLP Life Coach; a Certified Spiritual Healer; an Advanced Practitioner Reiki Master in Usui, Kundalini, and Lightarian healing modalities; a Holographic Memory Resolution trauma therapist, and a Healy Quantum Healing energizer. Her motivation is simply to help people feel better. Her greatest passion comes from empowering others to see the world and themselves in a more positive light via the mind, body, and spirit. She's a master perspective shifter who facilitates awareness, healing, and permission to be your true authentic self. Beth draws on her strengths as an empath and intuitive to help her clients unfold and expand into the very best version of themselves. She adores her husband, three children, and precious Goldendoodle, Angel.

An "International Best-Selling Author," Beth penned **Beth's Case Scenario** and contributed to **Enduring Wisdom**, both available on Amazon. She currently offers one-on-one sessions, workshops, A.R.M.S. training courses, and Mind, Body, Spirit retreats.

Join Beth's community at www.SpeakToBeth.com
Contact: Beth@SpeakToBeth.com
www.Facebook.com/SpeakToBeth and
www.Instagram.com/SpeakToBeth.

Remember Who You Are

By Beth Eiglarsh

"Voices in your head versus whispers from the heart.
One criticizes; one crystallizes!" —Beth

When I was a little girl, I would visit my Aunt Greta and Uncle Dick in North Carolina and listen to their cosmic stories of their extraterrestrial encounters. Their home sat upon their mountain, surrounded by goats, a donkey, and a pair of lamas—Dalai and Karma. The inside of their house was a museum of magic. Everywhere I turned, my childlike eyes were met with crystals, melted spoons, wizards, ETs and UFOs. Experiences with other realms were a non-negotiable reality—one that I oddly felt both curious about and comfortable with from the very beginning. At my young and innocent age, my mind was wide-open. Excitedly, I absorbed their other-worldly wisdom.

When I was in my teens, Uncle Dick sat me down and shared a scenario that shaped my view of the world. His story explained *everything*. It clicked. It resonated. It was my subconscious understanding of life, realized.

"Imagine that you are a driver in an old car, maxed out at two-hundred-thousand miles. On its final journey, the decrepit, worn-out vehicle approaches a cliff. It peaks over the edge, about to plummet to its demise." He paused and asked me a profound question. "Would you go over the cliff with the car—or would you exit the car and get into a new vehicle?"

There it was! A crystallized awareness that we are not our bodies, just as the driver is not the car.

In the above metaphor, when the car—or your body—gets old, it "dies." The driver represents our soul—source energy uncontained, uninhibited, and a part of all that is. Where the flesh ages and limits our momentum over time, the soul grows brighter, fueled by the human experience. When we choose to incarnate, we remain that ball of light, housed by physicality. Those who remember this and tap into that essence within navigate their human journey with greater ease and grace. They feel and use that infinite flow of support and know they are never alone. Those yet to remember their very own power source, those who deem themselves to be their body, their face, their name, their career title, and their circumstances, fall prey to discourse, dis-ease and discontentment.

Unification of the body and soul is paramount to living a life with purpose—accessible through introspection and motivated by joy. This merger converts everyday "I have tos" into "I get tos." It reminds us to be grateful every day we can take a breath—even on days when it feels hard to breathe.

Your physical self accounts for a mere 5% of your existence, driven by your brain. The subconscious driver of your human vehicle represents the remaining 95%, powered by your heart—the home of your divine blueprint.

When we make our subconscious conscious, we reconnect to that everlasting part of ourselves that knows far more than we do. When you become quiet and set an intention to merge, you can hear what your soul needs. Those directives of inspiration are your internal GPS that steers your authentic voyage. Those messages are *whispers from the heart.*

Before you stepped into this human body, you were in a huddle with all those crazy relatives in your life (Yes, even your exes). You collaborated to determine how you would maximize your time here on earth. Standing in that soul circle, you crafted various scenarios to help you grow, evolve, and ultimately master a predetermined soul lesson. Free will dictates which course we adhere to or stray from, yet the options are outlined like multiple routes on a map. When we are born, we bring forth our previously-conquered evolutionary lessons to assist the world with our wisdom. We also appear with a healthy dose of forgetfulness so we can fully experience life.

How do we remember why we are here?

Pay attention to the whispers.

When you give your brain a rest and drop into your heart, you receive pure messages from the spirit world. The narrator of these messages could be your master guide, your spiritual support team, angels, your higher self, or God. When we are unaware of these sweet love notes, they escalate into SOS messages in a bottle that crash onto the shore with an unexpected tidal wave. When we ignore these messages, they get louder, the consequences of not hearing them get greater, and the crises we face become chronic and sometimes even life-threatening.

What if I told you it's not about those details ... or the crisis ... or the circumstances?

Messages are designed to get your attention when something requires a shift. Have you placed a limitation on what you're capable of becoming? Are you avoiding what you are being nudged to walk through? Are you delving into what you came here to achieve, even if that means achieving contentment?

As a reformed workaholic, I look back on my days of *never enough* as a big blur. I forgot that I was more than my accomplishments, and I measured my success and intermittent happiness by what others deemed successful. My designs were displayed all over the world and in the hands of hundreds of celebrities, but I was unhealthy, unhappy, and oblivious to the needs of those I loved, including myself. I thought joy could be found at the bottom of my to-do list. I was busy doing everything and nothing—caught up in a whirlwind of perfection, overwhelmed by the noise associated with my chaos. Afraid to slow down, I couldn't hear a thing:

A voice that would challenge the activity I was consumed with?

A cry for help?

Was I fueling a lifestyle that was carrying me farther away from my true calling?

My Heart Whisper

When the balls I was juggling finally fell, the inevitable crumble ensued, and life got quiet. In that silence, I rediscovered myself. It was there that I heard my soul whisper to me. The year was 2010, and I had just returned from Carlsbad, California, where I spent a week at the Deepak Chopra Panchakarma retreat, eating Ayurvedic food, getting coffee enemas, enjoying third eye activation massages, and learning to meditate.

When I returned home, I was excited to take my newly-found practice to a local park. I had learned to ask the universe, "What is my dharma, my purpose?" I settled in, closed my eyes, and posed the question. Without hesitation, I heard, "to spread love and compassion."

What? Was that real? Somehow, I knew it was. I had spent over four decades searching for who I was, and in that moment, I knew. I dropped my shoulders, took my first deep breath in years, and cried happy tears.

That day was monumental for two reasons:

1. I understood that I could hear a message from thin air, firmly intended for me.

2. That message changed the trajectory of my life. My seeking ceased as I knew I embodied all that I needed to be. On that beautiful sunny day at the park, I was handed the access key to an exponentially more fulfilling life.

Trust the Whispers

We are continuously bombarded with words we hear others speak, and that we mutter to ourselves. They are too loud, too convincing, and too believable. Listening to the heart requires faith. We wonder where the whispers come from, question their subtlety, and doubt the message. Trust is a gift that we offer the spirit world. When we trust that things will unfold as they are designed, we can be gentler on ourselves. When my head tries to convince me that I should be farther along than I am, my heart reminds me that I am exactly where I need to be.

While preparing for an upcoming retreat, my head kept exclaiming, *Why haven't you written your curriculum yet?* This one-sided authoritative dialogue continued: *People are expecting to learn something from you. What's wrong with you? Why can't you just sit down and develop your program?*

I got busy with other projects, and one day turned into the next. I began to notice that whenever I found a quiet moment—meditating, enjoying a cup of coffee, driving, taking a shower—the curriculum came to me. My subconscious handed me the pen and prompted the words. My mind that was trying to bully me took a vacation, and my heart whispered, *I've got you. We've got this!*

Afraid of The Whispers

As a life coach, I frequently hear complaints about jobs, spouses, and health challenges. In response, I bring the focus inward and examine where people might have abandoned themselves. "Where are you out of alignment with your core values?" "When was the last time you belly laughed?" "When was the last time you allowed yourself to be vulnerable?" "When was the last time you took 100% responsibility for your own happiness?" I convey that their challenging circumstances are divinely crafted to get their attention. Then we create an intentional action plan to overcome the hurdles and get back on track. When my clients believe they are the car, I remind them that they are the driver. Freedom is available once we realize we can open the door and walk in a new direction.

A client expressed how she hated her job. She was working with her ex-boyfriend—the boss—and she believed that he was the source of her distress and misery. I asked if she had considered finding a new place of employment, but she said it was easier to stay. Rationalizing staying stuck is like taking a warm bubble bath in dirty water. So many of us justify and defend staying stuck where we don't belong rather than taking a leap of faith into the unknown. Her sacral chakra—the energy center for joy, and her throat chakra—the energy center for self-expression—were depleted. Her heightened frustration was really with herself. Her ignored whisper had become a loud roar that she could no longer disregard. The message had little to do with her boss and more about an unhealthy environment that she'd outgrown. Her 5% screamed, *The problem is him.* Her 95% replied, *I made the situation with him so difficult, that you had to walk away.*

Earth Angel Whispers

As an empath and intuitive, I listen to spoken words, and also to what isn't said. When stuck in those blind spots, we can lean on those trusted few in our lives for clarity until we can see things clearly. When we are out of alignment with source energy, it can be helpful to receive divine messages of empowerment from those who have our best interest at heart. Something beautiful happens when we prioritize our well-being: earth angels show up to guide us.

Not long after that magical day at the park, I spent the day with a dear friend. I expressed my desire to use my experience, strength, and hope to be of maximum service to others. My friend had just received her certification as an NLP Life Coach. She asked me if I had ever considered that path and turned up the volume on my whisper. I signed up for the course the very next day.

Decipher the Whispers

Whispers from the heartbeat of the universe deliver the highest value for all. This unconditional love provides us with a palette for our individual canvas. Every brushstroke of effort makes our collective gallery more colorful, vibrant, and interesting.

Conversely, the voices in our heads threaten our developing masterpiece. Our inner critic points out our imperfections, condemns our progress, and forces us to question our abilities. *Did I really believe I could be the next Picasso? What was I thinking?*

Thinking takes place in our brains where we ruminate over our to-do lists, question the characters we play, and obsess about whatever crisis we are facing. There is value to that aspect of ourselves—until it blocks the unthinking part of us that is aware of our circumstances, yet not attached to them. If we practice non-thinking, we can drown out the noise and access that place that lies beyond thought, where the whispers live—that world where our beliefs, avatars, and challenges are illusions created to help us grow.

How do we know which is which?

Soul Whispers are pure, loving, comical, truthful, inspiring, empowering, and kind, but when avoided, they can grow loud, sarcastic, persistent, and annoying, even though they come from a place of love.

Head Voices are condemning, anxious, frazzled, spiteful, critical, or judgmental.

Honor The Whisper

We drown out the subtle messages when their directives seem impossible, unattainable, or just too difficult. A degree of safety is realized in avoiding that voice of reason. Starting something new can be scary, but you can only hide for a limited time before your sacred mission reveals itself—either quietly or quite *loudly*.

Embrace the agony that echoes that deafening public service announcement from within. Pain is your greatest ally, and it's your gateway to heaven on earth. The depth of the wound is equal to the degree of self-actualization. It's in that unchartered space where you transform. It's in that sea of vulnerability where you discover your superpower. It's in your story's intermission — *inner mission* — where you remember who you are. You will be presented with what you need for your soul's expansion. Honor that and use your growing pains as a springboard to attain new heights.

My Whisper To you

Look how far you've come! There was a time when you doubted your strength. Recall a painful time in your life and focus on the moment you became the hero. Identify a person or organization where you can use your story as a service opportunity. Your hardship will alchemize someone else's pain. Be their whisper.

My contribution to this book is a whisper from my heart to yours. Hear it. Feel it. Know it. Remember who you were before the world told you who to be, and fuel that part of your soul. Today. You deserve it.

WHISPER EXERCISES

1.   <u>Lose Your Mind</u>

Choose an *in*activity—meditation, coloring, gardening, yoga, journaling, dance, et cetera—to access your whispers. Give your brain a vacation and drop into your heart. Turn up the volume. Life is a balance between being and doing and giving and receiving. Take 30 minutes to be an open vessel and allow what comes. Jot down your experience.

Tip: Say *thank you*. Nurture that relationship with the heard and not seen.

_____

_____

_____

_____

2.   Mess or Message

Write out your current challenge. Tune into your internal dialogue. Are you perpetuating the mess you see with your brain? Or are you looking for the message you hear with your heart?

Challenge:

_____

_____

_____

What is your head saying?

_____

_____

Look beyond. Identify a positive intent of this challenge. List any benefits of this mess landing on your path. What do you stand to gain?

_____

_____

3.   Challenge The Voices

Talk back to your head. Before accepting that critical voice, ask yourself these simple questions: yes/no.

Is this kind?   _____

Is this true?   _____

Is this helpful?   _____

Is this necessary?   _____

Bonus: Now speak to yourself as you would to a best friend or your 8-year-old self.

4.   I Love Me

Whispers are the universe screaming. *Remember who you are*. Describe what you love about yourself. Then trick your brain by turning those assets into daily mirror affirmations.

I AM

_____

I LOVE

_____

I ADMIRE

_____

I VALUE

_____

I TRUST

---

5.   <u>Soul Awareness</u>

Instead of allowing your thoughts to dictate how you feel, decide how you want to feel and adjust your thinking. Become aware of the current emotions occupying your internal real estate. Identify them, embrace them, and release them. Create space.

State the following out loud. Let your soul finish the sentence. Refrain from judgment. Restart the phrase repeatedly, prompting your innate response, until nothing more arises.

"When I connect with myself deeply, I feel":

_____

_____

_____

_____

Decide how you want to feel.

Go make that happen.

Chapter

Five

Listening To My Lifelong Whisper
By Rina Escalante

Rina Escalante

Rina Escalante is a first-generation Salvadorian American from the San Francisco Mission District. Her family immigrated to San Francisco in the late '50s and early '60s. She became a single mother when her daughters were three and one year old and became a member of corporate America out of need, not want. Rina has fulfilled roles such as a Staffing Manager, Employee Relations Officer,

Corporate Trainer and Project Manager. Some of the volunteer capacities she devoted her spare time to were coaching youth soccer, Boys and Girls Club soccer tournament director, conducting presentations at welfare-to-work programs and created mentorship programs for at-risk high school students. Rina's life completely changed when she began having strokes in 2010. She has had three major strokes and had to relearn how to walk, speak and use her right arm and the function of her right hand. She also survived thyroid cancer in 2017.

The alpine lake and mountain air of South Lake Tahoe is where Rina has found peace and is continuing to discover her calling. She began writing stories during the pandemic of 2020. Rina believes that if you allow Spirit to surround you with positive energy and live your life in gratefulness, anything is possible. She shares her life experiences in her storytelling with the intention the reader will know they are not alone on their life journey and looks at her life as always moving towards the greater good for all.

Rina can be reached at sacredwitchtahoe@gmail.com.

Listening To My Lifelong Whisper
By Rina Escalante

Faith.

It is a topic I have touched on and written about before; however, I feel it cannot be spoken about enough. Nor the possibility of living a life where you learn to attune yourself to a belief in something that is constantly running behind the scenes and helps guide you to do the best you can for yourself. I have discovered that faith has the ability to help absorb that overwhelming burden I have felt in those toughest of spots I have found myself in. Faith has played a major role in my life journey and guided me through some very rough patches. In my eyes and in my heart, it does not matter nor make a difference who or what you believe in. My hope is that you believe in something that is greater than yourself.

In thinking about a definition for faith, I thought about what having faith meant to me and the feeling I get in return for having it because I know my faith has to do with that light inside of me. I do not remember a time in my life when I did not have absolute belief in God. A greater energy than I, that looked out for my greater good; I have always known it to be true and never doubted. The emotions I have felt that having faith has given me have ranged from absolute peace to tears of joy to relief to not have to carry a burden alone. The feelings of trust, reassurance and absolute confidence in God are how I would summarize my singular faith experience.

Faith:

1. confidence or trust in a person or thing; *(faith in another's ability)*

2. belief that is not based on proof *(He had faith that the hypothesis would be substantiated by fact.)*

I am confident that my **belief** in The Creator, God, Spirit, Divine Love Energy, The Universe, was already part of my soul being before I was born. Of that, I have no doubt. Nor do I remember a time growing up, where going to Church to visit God was not central to how I was being raised. Up through high school, I was involved in my Parish's Catholic youth group and would beg my dad (with the fervor of a teenage girl) to let me attend every Catholic youth retreat that came across our youth group's desk (sorry, Dad—and thank you!). As a young parent, I became a Catechism teacher and taught a special mixed-grade class of second and third-grade children. The third-grade children had never received any type of religious education and were also preparing for their sacrament of reconciliation and first communion (their religious foundation). The second-grade children were continuing on their religious education path and were on track for their sacraments as well. As an adult, when I had the time and ability, I used to attend Daily Mass and was an active parishioner.

The **grace** I feel faith gives is that it is a living part of us. Faith has the ability to grow and to wither based on how much effort we expend to nurture it. In an effort to live a harmonious life, working in communion with faith allows us to have the capacity to transform, and we allow it to transform us, depending on how much of a presence we allow it (Spirit) to occupy within.

To live in union with Divine Love has always been innate. *I have always felt it as a need;* this inner light, similar to a love energy or unconditional love *(the only way I can describe it)*, has always wanted to burst out of my soul being. Lucky for me, it came with a life skill, **empathy**.

"*Empathy* is about standing in someone else's shoes, feeling with his or her heart, seeing with his or her eyes. Not only is empathy hard to outsource and automate, but it makes the world a better place."

~ Daniel H. Pink, *author*

I would not describe being empathetic as a *reciprocal emotion*. Feeling/taking on others' emotions vs. comprehending and listening (which is all someone may want or need) has had its ups and downs. I have gotten walked on, inadvertently become an enabler, and abusive relationships are also, sadly, a risk of an unbalanced skill set when it comes to being an empath. Not putting yourself first, in order to make sure everyone else is happy, because that is what "makes you happy" is a regular occurrence for an empath. Appeasing others will drain your energy if you do not protect your spiritual self, impose boundaries on yourself and others.

Learning how to ground, dispel negative energy and to transmute that energy are necessary skills to develop, nurture and create as a daily practice if you are an empathy.

Clearing, cleansing, and transmuting negative energy can be done through sending out clear intentions. I clear and cleanse away any and all negative karmic energies, spirits, and entities. I ask that whatever is not mine to carry, to be returned from whence it came. I fill the empty spaces I have just cleared with love, positive energy, and white healing Angel light. I send the negative energies back to Mother Earth and ask that they be transmuted, and I visualize it becoming a beautiful meadow that nourishes nature, where it was barren, let life grow and give back for the greater good of all.

Your prime purpose in this life is to help others. And if you can't help them, at least don't hurt them. ~ *Dalai Lama*

My **instinct** is the light I have always felt within. They are the *whispers* I hear from Spirit; they guide me on a daily basis, and I work on listening to them daily. I haven't always listened, and on those occasions, the lessons have been a bit harder to swallow, but I truly feel that is where my lessons have been the most impactful and continue to teach and lead me to trust my instinct. They can be the smallest of decisions where I say to myself, "I should have listened to my instinct and made that left." Your instincts can also guide you against making a left turn on the path of life…

There are many other ways you can become more attuned to yourself and your instinct, but like with faith, working with your instinct should ultimately become part of your daily routine. Divination tools have become wonderful instruments for me on how to learn to listen to and be guided by my instinct. It has become a relationship based on trust and connection to Spirit and the purity of intention within me. I recommend practicing and using tools on a regular basis. There are so many to choose from, and using your instinct to develop a relationship with your tools really is a great way to uncover your intuitive gifts.

I have always prayed with ***intention;*** it is my preferred approach to all things. My modus operandi views 'tasks' (whatever they may be, ranging from cooking to making smudge sprays) as a process that has a necessity for fluidity (a flow) and everything is surrounded with their own energy and, as such, deserves my time and devoted attention. This skill is how I approach energy healing Reiki, how I cleanse and clear spaces, conduct readings or when I practice any type of rituals. Intention is everything.

Life's natural sync is all about balance, and it is that way with faith: *"If we have faith, what is it that we get in return?"* or *"where is the proof?"* For me, when I think about what I receive in return for having faith, my answer has always been pure, simple, and uncomplicated: "Happiness and peace in my soul and my heart." This is why you will, more often than not, find me smiling, laughing, and engaging others. As for proof? The fact that I survived all the illnesses of my childhood, am a survivor of three major strokes, thyroid cancer and had to relearn how to walk, speak, write, and basically relearn how to use my right hand, speaks volumes. The energy sent to me from friends and family during all those years of recovery has been unbelievable. I absolutely credit my recovery to the prayers and positive energy being sent to me.

I chose a long time ago to live in gratefulness and appreciation for my life every day. As a young mother, I was exposed to people that were bitter about their life's circumstances and miserable about the direction their life had taken. That experience taught me to make a conscious choice to live life with a positive outlook, not waste it being angry about what should have been, what should have happened and angry about past circumstances that could not be changed because it happened in the past. It just seemed like a waste of the gift of life in my young mind (thank goodness).

I am grateful that life lesson happened to me when I was a young parent as it taught me that my life is a gift, and I should accept it with gratitude, regardless of what bumps happen along my journey. This attitude has been my guiding light through all my medical challenges over the course of my life. Every day I make a conscious choice to always seek the positive out of life's situations, and no, it has not always been easy by any stretch of the imagination. Even when I was in my darkest of days, I knew; I had faith that things were going to get better, I had **no doubt**. I knew my faith, and the balance of the Universe would get me through to the other side where the situation would be improved, and if not at that exact moment, it eventually would.

The loving, compassionate and enveloping gift faith gives us is that there is no "one way" to "do" faith. Faith is very personal; it is a *practice*. The more you practice, the more you give to your practice, the more you will get out of it, and the more it gives back to you. It is personal to each person's belief system. Like with any relationship, the more you give to it, the more you get out of it; it is absolutely about investment.

Over the past 16 months, 2020-2021, humanity has been experiencing a pandemic similar to the plagues throughout the annals of history. In March of 2020, the entire world shut down, and all of humanity sheltered in, forcing our dependency on the Internet and our hand-held computers to fulfill our needs. I moved in accord with so many others and began to take online courses, and I still continue to do so to this day.

During this time of isolation from this unknown virus, I was blessed to begin to experience my Awakening, began to put together many of the puzzle pieces of my life and began to make sense of my life journey. Looking back at these 18 months, I feel I have accomplished a lot. I have immersed myself into taking varying types of classes, began the study of numerology and Angel number messages, reacquainting myself with my intuitive gifts, learning how to use different Divination tools, clearing, and cleansing energies from spaces, becoming a first-time author of five collaborative books with one more on the way (this one), and becoming part of the workforce for the first time in eleven years since my strokes and cancer recoveries. I am filled with gratitude to be having so much personal discovery during this introspective period in history.

I was on the verge of personal Awakening from the very first online class I joined and was overwhelmed with physical reactions by my intuitive emotions. I have always carried within me this knowing that I *came here* with a purpose, not knowing what it was, just that I knew I had a purpose and trusted that one day I would know what it was. The first classes I began to take were on energy healing Reiki with a group of mostly Catholic and Christian women. I do not remember how I ended up in this wonderful class, but I ended up calling these ladies The Congrega (coven). The name of our group was a message I received intuitively from the Divine (I call it *downloaded*). (We) The Congrega had truly developed a bond when it came to healing or guiding others through hardship as a unit, hence, The Congrega. I was amazed at how we worked so well as an "intuitive team." The foundation and importance of grounding was a gift of learning I received from The Congrega.

After taking Reiki I, II, III and other courses with The Congrega, I began to fervently take diverse types of intuitive courses so I could continue to re-discover my gifts from Source, which I had turned off in my 30's... Back then, I blocked all of my intuitive gifts because I had no idea how to handle all the messaging being sent to and through me from Spirit. Approximately 25 years or so ago, so much information was being downloaded to me from The Universe (the only way I can describe it) I was absolutely *overwhelmed*.

The only way I knew how to handle it was to shut off all the gifts I had at that time, and I have no idea how I did it. I did not know what it was called at the time; I just called it "diarrhea of the mouth from the beyond" because I could just be standing in the grocery store line, when all of a sudden, all these words would come out of my mouth, and I had no control over what was 'coming out.' After Spirit was done relaying the message, I would just put my hands over my mouth. I would apologize profusely and tell the person, "I guess the message was meant for you? I hope you know what it means and who it was from." This was the case with psychic messages, past-life messages. I knew how to read tarot cards and had no idea how I knew how to read decks; it was a very emotional and physically exhausting time in my life. My mind never shut off. My dreams were so vivid, I did not know if I was awake or asleep sometimes. I slept with journals next to my bed to write down my dreams. I had three specific dream books I used for reference to analyze my dreams so I could make sense of what they meant.

One eye-opening discovery during this life-transitioning process has been *reflecting* on terminology I have always used and the context in which I used it, even though I had always thought of myself as a Catholic lady. Words such as energy, lifetimes, and karma. "Did you *feel* that person's energy, or was that just me?" "I think that in my past life, I must have been a teacher and a healer." "I better be careful what I do; what you give is what you get with karma!"

I am thankful that I had always approached Catholicism with an open mind formed from Jesus' view, "love one another as I have loved you." Over the course of my life, I have taken those words to mean that I was to accept and love **everyone.** I have embraced this gift of accepting and putting forth unconditional love as a gift from Source as I continue to evolve as a spiritual person. This life metamorphosis has given me the opportunity to look back at my life, my gifts and how I have allowed the Divine to flow within me.

I am grateful I have always allowed Spirit to guide me; I will *allow* my faith to grow and flourish within me. The time is now ripe to begin to practice what I have learned and to apply all that the Divine has reawakened within me. I am looking forward to continuing to evolve so that I may ascend, which is my ultimate goal.

Chapter

Six

Whispers or Deafening Roars
By Anne Foster Angelou

Anne Foster Angelou

Anne Foster Angelou is happy to be alive in Seattle, WA, with her beloved spouse. She is grateful for her life, all of it. Thank you, Universe!

Email: fosterangelou@comcast.net.

Whispers or Deafening Roars
By Anne Foster Angelou

"The mind thinks, but the heart knows."

My heart is "Big" on diagnostic imaging, they say. It has been in my body since womb times. I have been aware of it through emotional challenges, both joyful and fearful. The heartbeats increase or decrease with my thoughts, feelings and emotions. I won't tire you with scientific explanations of what happens when we think and trigger our subconscious and then create an emotion that manifests with hormonal changes, release of cortisol and adrenaline. I am sad to say my heart has mostly had negative challenges of fear and sadness, seemingly more than a human could bear. That is until I hear of the life challenges of others whose life stories stun me. I wonder how they had the strength and courage to carry on. We all think that of each other, don't we?

My heart has also known joy from loving and being loved, from sexual pleasure, and from crazy, belly-cramping laughter. I love to see and enjoy the humorous side of being alive.

There are so many words and phrases for the heart: heart-wrenching, heart-stopping, heart to heart, bless his/her heart (although this one has a critical, pitying aspect), it touched my heart, I didn't have the heart to (fill in the blank), my heart wasn't in it, my heart was in my throat, and in a heartbeat. Then there are words for cardiac events—heart attack and irregular heart rhythm. My maternal grandparents died from heart attacks, and their medical records are not available to know specifically why. My grandfather died of a massive heart attack at age 54. The death certificate said, in part, arteriosclerosis. My grandmother manifested heart issues during her first pregnancy at age 21. When I was a teenager in her guardianship and care, she took digitalis. She had a few heart attacks in the 20 years I lived with her and died of a heart attack and undiagnosed diabetes at age 62 when I was 20. Their D.N.A. was passed on to their six children and then on to me. I don't remember my aunts and uncles struggling with heart disease, except one aunt who was diabetic.

I have acted from my heart for as long as I can remember. I am sensitive, sentimental, affectionate, easy to cry and easy to become attached to humans and animals. My strong and vivid memory keeps long ago recorded experiences close to the surface, easily accessible. That helps me to write "my stories." Along with my heartfelt way of relating to the world, I have also developed a feisty, outspoken, protective attitude and fearlessness for speaking up about what is wrong for me and others less able to defend themselves. Somewhere along the way, from the shy young woman I knew and thought myself to be, I became articulate and assertive. My heart is easily touched and allows me to speak in defense of the defenseless, whether or not it is "my business."

My early life was full of challenges in my family of origin: violence, alcoholism, mental illness, poverty and all that they imply. My heart pounded and pumped blood in response to fear and safety issues. That poor little organ was working overtime. Fear, anger, shame and guilt take a toll on the heart.

I enjoyed fairly good health in my youth and up through my late 30s and early 40s (except for dreaded menopause that was steadily approaching). Abandonment and rejection issues also caused my heart to work overtime—the death of my grandmother, who raised me until I was 20, the failure of my marriage ending in divorce at 27 and resulting in clinical depression. My depression also resulted in being fired from my job and my only source of income. Luckily, I was re-employed soon after. I had to be hopeful and courageous in a strange city and state where I knew only my ex-in-laws, neighbors, co-workers and newly acquired friends in the previous seven years after arrival. "I got by with a little help from my friends."

Maybe a timeline will help to understand the challenges of my heart, positive and negative:

I was born in 1943 to a WWII widow who was in no condition to raise me (mourning and inherited emotional issues). I was called a British War Orphan even though my mother was alive. Her mother raised me from birth to age 20.

Age 5 – Began performing/singing on stage, coached and promoted by my grandmother.

Age 8 – Witnessed significant trauma (violence) out of town on a family visit and adjusted to having a mentally ill aunt come to live with us who later recovered to live a long life.

Age 9 – Skipped 5th grade due to I.Q. test results (a good thing but a challenge)

Age 12 – Uncle "J" came to live with us after 7 years in prison; he was 28, and I was afraid of him with good reason.

Age 16 – Graduated from Catholic high school (1960) and entered my freshman year at the University of South Florida.

Age 18 – Met my first husband at U.S.F. (he was from Redmond, WA).

Age 19 – Moved across the country in 1963 to Seattle, WA from Tampa, FL. I didn't finish my degree (3 years only).

Age 20 – Married a week after John F. Kennedy was assassinated (1963). My grandmother died in 1964, 10 months after I left home.

Age 27 – Divorced in 1970 after several years of marital dysfunction.

Age 29 – Met my second husband in 1972; still together after 49 years. He is a native-born Greek and came as a foreign student. Our challenges were different cultures and languages.

Age 29 – Hired at Seattle Opera in the professional resident chorus for the next 20 years (1973-1993). I was 49 when my contracts ended.

Age 29 – Graduated with a B.A. in "The Art of Performance" from the University of Washington and toured the state performing in an original *commedia dell'arte* opera for children. My thesis was the completion of an Actor's Journal for the tour and included a professional radio recording.

Age 31 – Married Dimitri in 1974.

Age 33 – Went to visit my husband's family in Greece and stopped in England to meet my English father's family for the first time. My English grandmother died three weeks after I met her.

Age 33-45 – Challenged with fertility issues until exploratory surgery discovered damage from a Dalkon Shield (I.U.D.), resulting in a class-action lawsuit for 22 years. My final effort was micro-surgery to remove adhesions when age then became a factor. Now we just love everyone else's children!

Age 50 – 69 – Performed in my own a cappella vocal quartet, The Angelou Vocal Ensemble, with a roster of talented opera singing colleagues for hire at private engagements.

Age and dates? Not important. I sang as a member of the Seattle Symphony Chorale; soprano and alto, for eight years prior to 2010.

Age 67-77 – 2010 to present, Member of The Medieval Women's Choir. Performed at St. James Cathedral for Christmas and at other local parishes in Seattle until interrupted by COVID.

MY SAVING GRACES:

- Love

- Humor

- Theatrical and Musical Performance (my creative soul)

I was blessed with an attractive, pure singing voice and acting skills, for which I am grateful. I have had many years and opportunities to perform professionally and non-professionally where my heart was happy and fulfilled. My skills also include foreign language studies which enhanced my vocal performance: Latin, French, Italian, German, and Greek. Other languages not studied formally but coached were Sanskrit, Russian and Czech.

WHERE IS THIS LEADING?

Aha! In 1993, my last year at Seattle Opera, I began to have chest discomfort when singing and can-can dancing at the same time (The Merry Widow). I sought cardiac evaluation and was initially told it was high blood pressure, weight gain, and then that I had "an anomaly, an aberration, an irregularity." For 10 years, the same cardiologist could not figure it out. We were not a match, and she insisted weight was a problem and "let's face it, you and I know it ain't gonna (sic) happen (weight loss)." I explained that I was experiencing chest pain after seconds of exertion on a treadmill or neighborhood walks and that I was in tears from the discomfort. My normal became exhaustion and pain after seconds of exertion. I could not walk from my front door to the car without feeling like collapsing. I forced myself to walk alone or with my husband in the neighborhood, but my physical limitations caused stopping every few steps to catch my breath or to get a back massage in an attempt to relieve the pain. I was also experiencing pre-syncope (fainting) even while driving alone in the car, and I would have to pull over for safety. As I would begin to pass out, adrenaline would start pumping. When I went for medical examination, the episodes had passed, and there was no way to detect it in a diagnostic test.

FULL-TIME EMPLOYMENT, DRIVING AND USING A DISABLED PLACARD

The inability to walk more than a few feet qualified me for a disabled placard. I was previously riding the bus, and it took a half-hour to walk two blocks to my office, and that meant holding my hands on the walls of downtown buildings and then taking way too long to cross the street before the light changed.

One morning, a personal friend (an architect working downtown) came up behind me and said, "Anne, is that you?" He was shocked to see me struggling, and I was embarrassed to be seen. Another time when I was struggling up a steep hill returning from lunch, I was again hanging onto the building walls for support and stopped at an exit to a parking garage. A truck driver was exiting and shouted from his vehicle, "Lady, do you need help? Can I take you to the hospital? Whatever you need!" I must have looked ready to collapse.

When I had meetings in other buildings, my colleagues would walk, and I would have to take a bus. That was also embarrassing. My normal was abnormal, but I was just living with it and trying to survive.

I had several diagnostic tests with the first cardiologist until one day she said with her arms crossed, "I don't know what to do with you. You just keep getting worse." She referred me to the U.W. Heart Institute, thank God, to a cardiologist who had a specialty. After two visits and one simple echocardiogram, he diagnosed me with hypertrophic cardiomyopathy with obstruction and gave me my options: (1) Open heart surgery to remove overgrown heart muscle that was obstructing blood flow, (2) an ablation (not as effective or successful as the first option) or (3) medication (the least effective option). I was afraid but used to "my normal," so I continued medical checkups with my new cardiologist, who specializes in H.C.M. It is 80% genetic, and testing was not necessary since I have no children to inherit it. Before I changed doctors, there was a difference of opinion on a medication I was taking. The new cardiologist said it was contraindicated for hypertrophic cardiomyopathy and strongly urged me not to renew my Rx. When I informed the other cardiologist, she "fired" me and told me to transfer my medical records to the new doctor. Gladly!

After about two years, I experienced fluttering in my chest for hours, no pain, but with a little back pain. I tried to ignore it and wanted to attend a farewell tea party for a neighbor who was moving into a retirement home. After several hours and no change in symptoms, Dimitri drove me to the U.W.E.R. The physician told me, "You either have had, are in the process of having or are about to have a heart attack." Nitroglycerin did not work, and the blood test enzymes indicated a mild heart attack with minimal heart tissue damage. My new cardiologist asked, "Are you willing to consider that heart surgery?" I asked where it would be done, and he said, "I send all my patients with this condition to The Mayo Clinic in Rochester, MN." I asked why I had to go out of town, adding to the unknown. He said, "because here we have one surgeon who maybe does it once a month and there, they have a whole team of surgeons and staff who specialize in this kind of surgery."

REFERRAL TO THE MAYO CLINIC AND OPEN HEART SURGERY (SEPTAL MYECTOMY) – 2013

We both got brave, and I decided I didn't want to live so impaired anymore. However, I was afraid of dying in the surgery (1% mortality), and I thought I was too old (69). Dr. Owens said I was a good candidate with lungs, liver and kidneys all in excellent condition. We checked Medicare and Secondary Medical Coverage. I joked with the financial staff at The Mayo Clinic, saying, "I might survive the surgery and drop dead from the bill!" He cracked up. After all the bills were sorted out, I paid $75 out of pocket for an $80,000 surgery. Not a bad deal. My friend from Minnesota said we would really enjoy "Minnesota Nice," and I thought he was joking. He was serious. Everyone was friendly and helpful: strangers, medical staff, hotel staff, genuinely wanting to accommodate our every need.

We stayed at a Holiday Inn across the street from St. Mary's Hospital with a horrible free breakfast but nice staff and a clean room. We arrived at the wee hours of the morning. I was all bathed and prepared according to instructions, fasting from food and water, and with a brave attitude and hope. Dimitri had a long list of whom to call after the surgery. I have photos of myself pre-surgery, minutes before walking into the hall on my way to the O.R. I don't remember much, like how I got onto a stretcher. A Catholic priest in regular clothing placed his hand on my head, and we said the Lord's Prayer. I couldn't have communion (food). My sweetheart kissed me, and we reminded each other of our love. Prior to surgery and in consultation with the anesthesiologist, I requested pediatric intubation to protect my vocal cords. She did that, and I had no throat or vocal cord damage or pain.

ICU AND RECOVERY

Dimitri witnessed my first toe wiggle prompted by the nurse, and he took a cell phone photo of me all wired and tubed because he knew I'd want to see that. After five days, they released me from the hospital, and I said, "What? I can't even get out of bed!" They taught me how to do that and after one night at the hotel, I was very sick and had no energy and couldn't even unscrew a medication bottle cap. We called an ambulance, and the staff informed me that I was in atrial fibrillation. The E.M.T. said he could give me a drug that would stop it and asked for my permission to do so. I spent two hours in the Mayo E.R. with a medication change, and the A-fib stopped, and I was running around thanking everyone and telling them to have a great day. I thanked all my caregivers, and one nurse and I cried when we said goodbye to each other. The Mayo has a gorgeous chapel with Italian marble. Dimitri took me there in my wheelchair to see this beautiful place.

RETURNING HOME

We had only one-way tickets because we didn't know how long we would be in Rochester with complications. Our return tickets cost four times as much as coming. A rude flight attendant reprimanded me for putting my stocking feet on the plastic bulkhead wall. My ankles were so swollen and uncomfortable, and I only did it for a few minutes with clean feet. I complained to her supervisor by pulling open my shirt to show the zipper stitches on my chest. He was apologetic but said something awkward like, "As a guest, I probably wouldn't put my feet on someone's furniture." What an idiot!

At Sea-Tac airport, I felt the impact of every bump my wheelchair encountered. Then the elevator to take us to baggage claim was not working, so I sat there in tears while Dimitri went to get help. Some returning passengers came over to see what I needed and called an airport manager. We finally arrived home to our friend and cat/house sitter and three beloved cats. Recovery was about three months until I could drive alone. Dimitri was on alert for my every need, and I had to sleep in the guest bedroom because the bed was lower. I was helpless and needed to be lifted out of bed and helped to the bathroom. I remember the joy of my first shower.

MY LIFE WAS PROLONGED – I AM GRATEFUL

I can now walk without pain or exhaustion, even for a few miles and for more than an hour. God bless the heart muscle that is no longer in my body. I am thankful for its support all my life until it was time to go. A Psych-K practitioner helped me say goodbye and allow it to be released.

Every day is a blessing. I will enjoy my life and continue to love and forgive, appreciating all those with whom I have shared my life, past and present. Dimitri's love and life-sharing is the greatest gift.

Chapter

Seven

When You Know, You Know
By Karen Gabler

Karen Gabler

Karen Gabler is an attorney, intuitive mentor and psychic medium. She is also a best-selling author, teacher and sought-after inspirational speaker. Karen is passionate about encouraging others to find their highest purpose and live their best lives. She mentors her clients through a variety of personal and business questions, marrying her practical legal and business experience with her intuitive ability to receive information and guidance from higher sources. She also facilitates connections with clients' loved ones in spirit. Karen conducts workshops, spiritual services and presentations on a variety of business, spiritual and personal development topics.

Karen earned her Bachelor of Science degree in psychology from the University of Hawaii and her Juris Doctorate from the William S. Richardson School of Law at the University of Hawaii. She has pursued wide-ranging education in interpersonal development and the spiritual sciences, working with tutors from the prestigious Arthur Findlay College for the Psychic Sciences in England as well as with intuitives and psychic mediums throughout the United States.

Karen is a WCIT in the Martha Beck Wayfinder life coaching program. She taught transcendental meditation as a student teacher at the University of Hawaii, and a variety of employment law courses as an Adjunct Professor at the Pepperdine School of Law in Malibu, California. Karen has published her stories in eight internationally best-selling collaborative books. She enjoys writing, reading, hiking, horseback riding and spending time with her husband and two children. You can find more information about Karen at www.karengabler.com.

When You Know, You Know

By Karen Gabler

"Y" ou'll know the truth when it feels good." "When you listen to your intuition, you'll feel yourself moving toward your dreams." "You'll find peace of mind by listening to your heart." There are thousands of quotes about listening to our intuition — that little voice inside our heads and our hearts that tells us where to go or what to do. Too often, these quotes seem to imply that because your intuition always guides you in the right direction, its guiding light should always feel good. The reality is that listening to your intuition may be the right thing to do, but that doesn't mean it will always be easy.

In 1996, I had been living in Hawai'i for ten years. I loved my life there, and had no plans to leave. I had a beautiful home with a backyard pool where I lounged with my dogs, who enjoyed their daily soak on the pool steps. My house was located two blocks from Kailua Beach, where I walked along the gently-rolling waves every morning. It was a home I inherited from my mother after she passed away two years earlier, and I found it comforting to live in a place that brought to mind my favorite memories with her. I was close with a group of friends who held my heart in their hands; we logged hundreds of hours together, laughing and crying over our life events. I was only two years out of law school at the University of Hawai'i and had landed a coveted associate attorney position at one of

Honolulu's oldest and largest law firms. I was relaxed and happy.

When my friend Ann moved from Hawai'i to Seattle to be closer to her family, I planned a weekend trip to visit her in her new home. I arrived to the stereotypical downpour of rain and marveled at the hustle and bustle of the city. The streets were packed with cars, and throngs of people walked in every direction. Tall evergreens replaced the palm trees I was so used to seeing on the horizon at home. Mount Rainier was majestic in the distance, and I was momentarily shocked to see the whiteness of snow on its peaks.

Ann deftly guided her car into a tiny parking space in front of a busy restaurant and said, "You'll love this place! Seattle has great food!" As I climbed out of the car and ran under a nearby awning, I turned to look at the city lights sparkling in the rain. Ann ran to join me and said, "So, what do you think of Seattle so far?" As I began to remark upon how different the city seemed as compared to the quiet island where our friendship had begun, an almost imperceptible thought fluttered across my mind.

It's time to move to the mainland.

I dismissed the thought as quickly as it came, and enjoyed the rest of my weekend with Ann. As my returning flight approached my much-loved island home, I stared through the plane window, marveling at the beauty of the mountains and the ocean. The flight attendant's lilting voice matched her sunny smile as she said, "Welcome to Hawai'i!" As I stepped out of the plane into the warm trade winds, smelling the sweet perfume of ginger and gardenia, another thought flitted across my mind.

I'm going to miss living here.

I was immediately saddened at the idea of leaving my home, and wondered where on earth these thoughts were coming from. I shook it off, telling myself I certainly wasn't leaving Hawai'i!

A few weeks after my Seattle excursion, a recently-hired senior attorney in my law firm called me into his office. Closing the door behind me, he shared that his kids weren't happy with their move to the islands, and he was planning to return to his law firm in California. He relayed that his firm had invited him to bring some of his talented associates back to California with him, and asked me if I was interested in a move. I told him I wasn't planning to move, but promised to think about it. Later that weekend, my then-boyfriend excitedly informed me that he had been offered an opportunity to work on a television show in Los Angeles. After months of trying to find work on a few random commercials filming in the islands, the prospect of moving to find steady film work was enticing.

I sat in the warm sand at my favorite beach, feeling the cool waves roll onto my feet and wondering why I kept thinking about moving away from my beloved home. As my mind threw out reason after reason to stay, my heart quietly and gently responded.

"I can't leave here. This is my home!"

Home is where you make it.

"But my mother was here! All my memories are here! I live in her house!"

She is always with you, wherever you are.

"I have a good job! I've worked hard for this career!"

Yes, you have. That's why you have a job opportunity waiting for you in California.

"All my friends are here! All my activities are here!"

Yes, they are. They will be here for you, but there are friends and activities there, too.

"But I LOVE IT HERE!"

I know. We will miss it, won't we?

As time moved forward and I argued with myself about leaving Hawai'i, more signs appeared to confirm that I was on the right path. A Hawai'i friend said he had a sister-in-law in California who was looking for someone to rent her home in Los Angeles for a year while she was traveling. A colleague offered to buy my car and some of my furniture if I moved away. A real estate agent sent a solicitation letter, noting that she had a client who wanted to live in my Hawai'i neighborhood and asked if I was interested in selling my home. I began to wrap my head around the idea of leaving the island, while still wondering if I had lost my mind.

At the same time, some people tried to discourage me. Another real estate agent told me that it would be a terrible mistake to sell my Hawai'i home; prices were rising, and I would never be able to afford another one. The moving company informed me that it would take close to a month to ship my belongings to the mainland; I would be living out of a suitcase for far longer than any vacation I had ever taken. My younger sister (who had become like a daughter to me after our mother passed away) called from her mainland college dorm room and complained that I was taking away her home; she begged me to stay in Hawai'i. And yet, as each obstacle presented itself, the small voice inside me grew stronger.

While preparing to put my house on the market, a friend was helping me paint my kitchen. Suddenly, I began to cry, still wondering if I was making a mistake. I began to list all the reasons why moving would be foolish. After listening to my rant, she gently said, "You know, you don't have to move if you don't want to." The words jumped out of my mouth: "Yes, I do! I do have to move! I have no choice!" I listened to myself argue with her, realizing that the voice inside me had already made the decision. No matter how difficult it might be, my intuition told me that it was time to go.

Swiss psychiatrist Carl Jung said, "Intuition gives outlook and insight; it revels in the garden of magical possibilities." Intuition is the opportunity to develop an immediate understanding, without resorting to conscious thought. It is often described as a "gut feeling," or the feeling of just knowing something without thinking about it. It reflects the voice within you; your internal compass that guides you to your next step or decision. Whereas our five senses of hearing, tasting, touching, smelling and seeing rely upon data derived in the physical world, our sixth sense – intuition – relies upon our internal world to facilitate a deeper understanding of our innermost selves.

Intuition can be loud on occasion, such as when you feel pushed out of the way to avoid an accident, or you just seem to know exactly how to escape a dangerous situation. Most of the time, however, it is an almost imperceptible whisper inside you. In the rush of daily life, it can be challenging to hear that internal voice – and yet, it is crucial that we develop the ability to do so. Albert Einstein said, "The intuitive mind is a sacred gift, and the rational mind is a faithful servant. We have created a society that honors the servant and has forgotten the gift." Living our best lives, with a full understanding of our soul's purpose, depends upon our ability to listen to the voice within rather than dwelling on the distractions around us.

Learning to listen to that whisper takes time, patience and practice. One of the best ways to begin connecting with your inner voice is to intentionally quiet the external noise. Taking time to meditate can open the door to communicating with your soul. Start with five minutes of silence, focusing on your breath. When your mind dwells on random thoughts, gently release them and return to focusing upon your breathing. You will find that deeper feelings arise from your soul when you sit quietly and allow them to bubble up.

If you find it challenging to sit in stillness, try walking in nature, sitting at the beach or listening to the wind in the trees. Connecting with the natural power that exists all around us, in a manner that allows you to just drift with your thoughts, can open the door to a closer connection with yourself. Even driving in silence, instead of turning on your favorite playlist or podcast, can give your intuition the time and space to connect with you.

Journaling in a stream of consciousness also can help you to connect you with your intuition. When you write freely, without editing or censoring yourself, you can set aside your mind and begin a conversation with your soul. Jot down a question you may have about your life, and write about how it makes you feel. When faced with divergent choices about how to proceed, write a short story about how each choice might unfold. Feel how you react to each story, and which choice pulls at your heart.

It also can be useful to spend time focusing on the sensations of your body, instead of the thoughts in your mind. Sit quietly and deepen your breathing. Feel for any areas of stress or tension in your body, and gently relax those areas. As you focus on your breath and feel a sense of calm filling your body, bring your mind to a question you have about your life. As you ask your question, notice how it feels within your body. Do you feel tense or stressed once again? Do you feel relaxed or energized? Paying close attention to your body's physical response to a question can give you key information about your innate reaction to your thoughts.

After you've learned to access your physical reactions, begin listening for the language of your intuition. Again, quiet your mind and focus on your breath. Ask yourself a question, and notice the first response that drifts into your mind, without conscious thought or analysis. You may find that you feel or hear an answer to your question even before you have finished asking it. Your intuition knows the questions bubbling up inside of you, and is prepared to answer them for you. The key is to listen to the immediate, almost subconscious response you receive, before letting your mind take over. This gut-level response is more likely to be your "true north," rather than the thoughts that come to mind after your rational side loudly inserts itself into the discussion.

Whatever method you choose to allow your intuition to express itself, the key is to trust that small inner voice when you feel or hear it – even when it seems to be telling you something you don't want to hear, or raises thoughts that come as a surprise to you. It is remarkably easy to listen to yourself when you open the door to doing so, but we are also too quick to ignore or disregard that voice inside us. This may occur when we don't trust ourselves, or because we are bowing to peer pressure or societal expectations. In reviewing the places in my life where I felt as though I had wandered off course, it typically occurred when I chose not to listen to my gut feelings, stubbornly insisting on doing what my mind thought I wanted instead of following my heart. Where I have followed the messages from my intuition, even when doing so seemed like it would be odd or difficult, it has always led me to unforeseen blessings and opportunities.

At the same time, it is important to remember that those blessings and opportunities may not be evident when your intuition first speaks to you. The guidance you receive may not immediately spark joy within you. Your intuitive "hits" should feel *right*, even if they don't necessarily feel *good* in that moment. I certainly didn't react with joy when my inner voice first told me to leave Hawai'i. Sometimes, your intuitive guidance can feel like you have scheduled yourself for surgery – you don't really want to do it, but you know it is the right thing to do. Your mind may try to "help" by offering a variety of roadblocks borne out of fear, stress or apprehension. Quiet your mind, listen in the stillness, and trust in your inner voice. Remember that your intuition will never steer you in the wrong direction. It has your best interests at heart, and it is here to keep you moving forward on your path.

Since my move to the mainland twenty-five years ago, my life hasn't been without its challenges, of course. And yet, the ensuing years have proven to me time and time again that following my intuition and moving to California, no matter how difficult it might have been at the time, was the right turn on my path. In California, my career blossomed and I earned more than twenty awards for my professional achievements. I rediscovered a childhood love of horses and finally had the resources and open land available to have several of my own, winning a variety of ribbons in our show jumping competitions. As I had done in Hawai'i, I became close with a group of friends who held my heart in their hands; we spent hundreds of hours together, laughing and crying over our life events. I found a beautiful home and decorated it with photos of my memories on my island and with my mother. Most importantly, I met the love of my life: a born-and-raised California man, who had never visited the islands. We built a family together, joyfully raising two remarkable children. Although my current life bears little resemblance to my prior island existence, it is also the same in one important respect: I am still relaxed, and still happy.

Ten years after my move to California, I took my husband to Hawai'i for his first visit to the islands. As our flight approached Honolulu, I stared through the plane window and marveled at the beauty of the mountains and the ocean. The flight attendant's lilting voice matched her sunny smile as she said, "Welcome to Hawai'i!" We stepped out of the plane into the warm trade winds, smelling the sweet perfume of ginger and gardenia. I thought about the day I moved away from this majestic place, and about the power of my intuition and the blessings that came from listening to that quiet voice inside me. My husband took my hand, and I smiled up at him with gratitude. I was thoroughly relaxed, and extremely happy.

Chapter

Trust the One Who Knows
You Best
By Sarah Gabler

Sarah Gabler

Sarah Gabler is 15 years old and in the tenth grade. She loves playing games with her family and traveling to new places. Sarah enjoys playing the ukulele and guitar, singing and dancing, and riding her horse. As a lifelong artist, she is pursuing a scholastic pathway in graphic design and loves using creative outlets to express her artistic vision. She is a technical sound artist for her high school productions and enjoys helping to bring a production to life to entertain others. She loves empowering people by helping them to recognize their true potential in the world and plans to do motivational speaking in the future. Sarah began exploring spiritual teachings and soul empowerment concepts when she was 10 years old and believes it has made her a better person today. It also has motivated her to find ways to live her best life and to help others on their journey to live their best lives as well. Sarah believes that even the smallest act of kindness can make someone's day, and she enjoys going out of her way to make others feel loved. Sarah dedicates this article with love to anyone who is having trouble trusting that voice inside of themselves.

Trust the One Who Knows You Best

By Sarah Gabler

Everyone has intuition. It is your guide, inner voice, friend, and much more. Your intuition can keep you safe, give you advice, and be your own personal angel on your shoulder. Many people don't know how to access their intuition. Some people listen to that little voice inside of them but don't know that the voice is their intuition. There are two sides to using your intuition: one is learning about what it does for you and how to listen to it, and the other is having the courage to listen to it, even in tough situations.

When I was very young, I was somewhat familiar with the concept of listening to myself when I needed to make decisions or when I occasionally felt guided to take my life on a certain path. At that time, however, I didn't really know it was called my "intuition." Then, when I was seven years old, I experienced a moment in my life that would change my perspective about my intuition forever.

I went on a walk with my mother and father around our neighborhood. We were on our way toward home, on the sidewalk about three streets away from our house. I was warm from walking up a hill, and my jacket was tied around my waist. With the boundless energy of a child, I was dancing around as we walked. As we reached a crosswalk in our neighborhood, I suddenly felt an overpowering urge to untie and re-tie my jacket. I was surprised at first because my jacket wasn't falling off my waist. Even though it felt secure, I just couldn't shake the feeling that it needed to be re-tied. I stopped to take my jacket off and insisted that my parents stop to wait for me. We stood at the edge of the crosswalk for about two minutes while I re-tied my jacket. I grabbed my parents' hands, and we stepped into the street.

It was a quiet morning, and no one was out. The only noise was the birds in the trees. Suddenly, a gray car came screeching around the corner. It sped past us in the middle of the crosswalk, making no effort to avoid us and ignoring the bright red stop sign at the corner. I could feel a gust of wind whip my hair as the car flew past us. Its tires squealed through the turn and raced down the street.

I stood there trembling, feeling paralyzed with terror. I couldn't even comprehend what had just happened. I had been looking down at the ground, holding my parents' hands, enjoying our walk, when suddenly, my parents were yelling and yanking me back out of the street. I was in a fog of confusion and shock.

We all caught our breath as my parents held me close to them. The car sped by so close to us! If we were just a few more inches into the crosswalk, we would have been seriously injured, if not killed. If I had not stopped to re-tie my jacket, I would have been hit by the speeding vehicle. We walked on in silence, tightly holding each other's hands. The rest of the way home, I was replaying that moment in my mind over and over again.

I firmly believe that the nagging feeling I had about needing to stop and re-tie my jacket was my intuition. My soul was protecting me and giving me an opportunity to choose whether I wanted to continue with this life. If I had said no to the call of my intuition that morning, I would have ended my journey on earth that day.

That experience taught me a lot about myself. It sparked my interest in the "other world," my understanding of my soul, and the process of connecting with my intuition. My intuition has influenced my life regularly since that day, and I have worked to keep getting closer and closer to my inner self. I strive to keep working with my intuition to become more self-aware and to make better decisions for myself and my family.

One of the methods I use to become more connected with my intuition is spending quiet time alone. I find that spending time by myself helps me to get my thoughts in order. I like to have no noise and no distractions, and then I lay down and let my thoughts run free. I think about the day I'm having, the days coming up in my life, how other people might be feeling, how I'm feeling, and anything else that comes up. I find that just letting my thoughts run in and out of my head helps to reduce my stress, increase my mental and emotional capacity, and have deep conversations with myself.

I also practice using my intuition every day, so I can strengthen that connection. Using your intuition to make simple decisions for yourself throughout the day, such as what to eat or buy or wear, can help to increase your trust in yourself and your inner voice. I also use my intuition to guide me in knowing what I need when I need to take care of myself. Sometimes, being in groups of people can be overwhelming for me. My intuition will tell me that I need to take a mental break before I become overly anxious or unhappy. I find that when I listen to that inner voice, I feel the happiest and healthiest that I can be.

In the rush of daily life, however, it can be hard to hear your intuition, especially when you are in a group of people or distracted by outside factors. It can also be difficult to remember to listen to your intuition when peer pressure becomes louder. It is easy to be drawn into the human need to be 'liked" or wanting to feel included. I sometimes get sucked into that feeling as well. Most of the time, that moment of losing touch with yourself and turning your attention outward instead of inward is when you most need your intuition. It is important to develop the confidence to listen to yourself and put yourself first. Sometimes, it takes time to get to that point.

When I first started middle school, I didn't know a lot of people in my class. I had one particular friend that I really liked and trusted in my sixth-grade year. We were buddies on field trips and best friends during lunch and in our classes. She was so much fun! Over the next few months, we met other incoming sixth graders, and we formed a small group of nice friends that we liked and with whom we felt safe. Everything was great for a while with my little group. I felt liked, I felt secure, and I felt included.

That warm feeling lasted until a new girl transferred to my school several months into the year. She was drawn to our group right away, and we welcomed her into our little circle. We encouraged her to join us at lunch every day because we all knew what it was like not to know anyone. She seemed shy and didn't speak much but seemed friendly at first. For a few months, we were a great group, and we all blended together very well. And yet, I couldn't shake the feeling that something wasn't right. Even though she seemed nice, I felt as though the new girl in our group couldn't be trusted.

Well, my intuition proved to be correct. After being part of our group for only a few months, she began working hard to become very close to my best friend. I began to feel as though she was trying to push me out. I would join a circle of my friends and ask what they were talking about, and she would say it was "a secret," and they couldn't tell me. I would get my lunch in the cafeteria and try to sit with my group, but she would tell me that there wasn't room for me at the table.

This was annoying, but it wasn't until a few months later that things really started to escalate. She began to spread unfair rumors about me, telling my friends that I had said mean things about them even though it hadn't happened. My whole group began to ignore me and leave me out of inside jokes and events. I felt completely invisible. They would whisper about me in their little huddles when I walked away, and they would move my belongings to another seat in the classroom so they could sit together and leave me out. On Valentine's Day, when my "friends" handed out chocolates and roses to the class, I was the only one who did not receive anything from them. That new girl that we were so kind to let into our group had turned my friends against me and was making my middle school experience a living hell. My original group that I called my "friends" were now my foes, and I did not know how to move forward.

I continued to ignore my intuition for a while and tried to remain close to them. I still called them "friends" for the longest time and took whatever tiny bits of attention I could get from them. I ate lunch with these "friends" for the rest of the year and tried to overlook every snarky comment, look, rumor, and action they threw at me. My intuition screamed at me every day to leave the group, but I just couldn't because I truly believed I didn't have anyone else. Now and then, I tried to sit with other classmates to separate myself from my toxic group, but I just couldn't seem to find my way into any other groups. I always seemed to feel out of place, and I came home crying every day because of the way my "friends" excluded me.

Finally, I just became too fed up to take it any longer. I was frustrated with their comments and ridicule and tired of ending each day in tears. I was finally ready to be done and decided I would end these toxic friendships that day. My intuition whispered its guidance to me throughout the morning. I told myself, "You are going to be alone for a while, but it's okay. You are strong. It is good to be alone!" I had to accept that staying in the group wasn't healthy for me and acknowledge that my mental health had been plummeting ever since that new girl joined my circle. I needed to make a strong decision for myself, and I needed to put myself first. No more burying my intuition deep inside me because of fear. It was time…way past time!

I walked from the lunch line to where the group sat to eat. Inevitably, some of the girls in the group ignored me once again, and one of them made another rude comment toward me. I felt all the frustration and resentment I had been holding inside of me. I had been building up so much emotional damage caused by that group, and I was ready to burst into tears. Every day, I had been voluntarily walking into a lion's den just to be torn apart all over again. I told them that they used to be such nice people but had somehow become rude and cruel. I told them that I went home crying every day because they made me feel worthless. I told them to think about how it felt to be in my shoes. I watched their faces turn from smug to shocked and noticed several of them lowering their heads in shame.

That day, I left the entire group for good, even the few remaining people that I still liked. Several of them later told me privately that they were sorry and wished they had not gone along with the group. They told me that they hated the toxicity of the group as well. I explained that it would be healthier for them if they left the group and remained true to themselves instead of going along with the crowd. They agreed but didn't feel strong enough to leave. I was proud of myself for finally listening to my intuition and saving myself. I had done what I needed and was able to do, and I was free.

Although that was a horrible experience for a 12-year-old, it made me a much stronger person. I became so much more mature, empathetic and self-aware. It reminded me of the importance of listening to that quiet voice inside me before it turns into a scream. I can now say that listening to my intuition (even though it took many signs to get there) was once again the best decision I could make. I also know that I would have had a lot more fun in middle school if I had listened to my intuition earlier. I learned that even when it is scary, and even when it feels like everything around you will crumble, it is so important to listen to the voice of your soul. It will always lead you to a healthy and powerful decision that will benefit your life forever.

I have been through many other experiences with my intuition, and I haven't always listened as closely as I should. In every situation where I have ignored my intuition, it has delayed my path forward or caused me emotional pain. Now, at age 15 and as a sophomore in high school, I have learned to listen to my intuition right away, rather than second-guessing it. My current school year began a little over a month ago, and my intuition has already guided me away from groups that I now know would have been toxic for me. I am friends with a great group of people that I enjoy, who love me and want me around them, but I know I have the strength to rely upon myself whenever necessary. I have used my intuition to make smarter decisions throughout the school day, such as how to approach my schoolwork, when I need to ask for help, and when to walk away from a situation that isn't right for me. When I use my intuition, I feel more grounded and more connected with my inner self, and I feel as though I am secure and guided in my journey.

There will always be ups and downs in life. I've had mine, without a doubt, and I know there will be more. Without my intuition, I would be lost, and it would take me much longer to return to my true path. I honestly don't know where I would be if I didn't have my intuition to guide me. I certainly would be more stressed, and I would be unsure and insecure about how to navigate my life. By trusting my intuition, I now know how to make better choices for myself, and I am in a much healthier place. My intuition is my most powerful tool, and it keeps me safe mentally, emotionally and physically.

To become familiar with your intuition and learn what it can do for you, I would suggest embracing it on a regular basis. Try to be more self-aware, even in the midst of chaos. When making decisions about which way to turn on a street or which piece of merchandise to buy, try quieting your mind and asking your intuition what you need in your life at the moment, and see how it works out. It might end up being a decision that changes your life. When dealing with a tricky situation, feeling pressured by those around you, or struggling with a decision, your intuition is your inner guide. It will always help you find your way back home, wherever your home may be.

Chapter

Nine

Scouts Honor
By GG Rush

GG Rush

GG Rush is a perpetual student and seeker of knowledge, experience and enlightenment. She is a "Wayfinder Life Coach In-Training." She attended "Martha Beck's African Star Program" at Londolozi Game Reserve in South Africa. She is certified Reiki II and is studying Reiki III under Master Marina Lando MS, who has also taught her Aromatherapy, Chakra Balancing, Toxic Emotions and the ancient art of Pulse Reading. She has traveled the world solo and will continue her journey to see the world and find herself. GG, aka Gail Rush Gould, resides in Cary, North Carolina, with her cat Bella.

Scouts Honor

By GG Rush

I was sitting last night, talking to my daughter Rachel about our adventures in Girl Scouts over the years. Both of my daughters Rachel and Sean Elizabeth were Scouts. Rachel started with Brownies and Sean with Daisy's. They both stayed until Seniors or Ambassadors, which was when they were in High School. At the end of their tenures as Scouts, they each received, as a gift from me, a Lifetime Membership, so forever Girl Scouts. I was never officially a Leader, but I was a Cookie Mom for years, and I did ten years as a Day Camp Leader for one week each summer. That was how I spent my summer vacation from work. Always in June and hot, humid and muggy outside from early morning until late afternoon.

I was a Brownie and Junior Girl Scout in my youth, and I loved it. Many fond memories, so when we discovered that a Brownie Troop was forming at Cary Elementary, I was quick to enroll Rachel in the troop. I don't remember much about that first year, except I raised my hand when they asked for a volunteer for Cookie Mom. I had no clue what I was getting into. We had a blizzard with record snow during the first week of sales. Rachel was adorable in her winter coat with her Brownie beanie on top of her long curly hair. She walked our neighborhood and charmed every single house into buying multiple boxes. After all, we were all stranded because, in the south, one snowflake means 'shut down,' but a blizzard means stranded. One

114

particular house at that time was occupied by a group of just graduated college guys, and I think they bought five cases! So once we got close to the delivery day, as I tallied the numbers, I realized the entire troop had sold a record number of cookies. I had to recruit four moms with minivans to go to the fire station for pickup. Once we got to my house with the cookie cases, and there were hundreds, we turned my living room into a cookie warehouse. It was like a maze of stacked cookie cartons. Thin Mints here, Samoas in this sector, Trefoils here. I had to keep spreadsheets so when the girls and their parents came for pick up, I could accurately sort their orders. It was daunting, but I loved it. They made a huge amount of money, and the girls were so proud. I did Cookie Mom a few more times over the years, but after that first round, I tried not to raise my hand ever again.

Sean officially started as a Daisy in Kindergarten. This was because, from day one of seeing her big sister in her Brownie uniform, Sean wanted to be a Scout. She actually cried and said, "I want to be a Girl Scout too, Mommy!" I didn't know about Daisy troops at the time, but we quickly found out and enrolled her. Her original Troop Leader, Ms. Robin, was her leader from Daisy troop to Ambassador troop. But Sean's first real troop was Pixie's. This brings me to Day Camp memories.

Being included in the hard-to-get-into local Day Camp was a difficult task. When I found out both of my daughters would be accepted if I volunteered, it guaranteed Rachel would get into a Brownie group. So, of course, I raised my hand. Sean, at that time, a toddler in diapers, would be accepted as a Pixie. So basically, being babysat all day while I could be a leader. I was assigned to a Brownie division, and Rachel was in my group. Often time I had to dodge Sean because if she saw me, she would cry. That first year there were no themes or a lot of ideas, but the week was full, and we had the luxury of being at an Elementary school, so we had some time in the air-conditioned cafeteria. At the end of the week, I was exhausted, had two exhausted young daughters and was thinking this was our last time doing this. And on Friday, at the closing ceremony, it was my birthday. They surprised me with a cake and over 200 girls singing "Happy Birthday" to me. I cried so hard and thought, "Well, I guess I am hooked now. I should mention the opening and closing ceremonies every day." Each group would have an opportunity to do an opening and closing flag ceremony every morning and every afternoon. Seeing even my little Pixie show pride in carrying a flag and reciting the pledge was priceless. After that first year, we moved to a local park and stayed outside from then on.

Over the 10 years at Day Camp, we grew as women. Each group was assigned a Program Aide (PA) who were older Senior scouts. The PAs always went by camp names, and at the end of the week, they would do a skit and finally give their real names to the delight of the younger campers. Over the years, I had Sunshine and Luna at different times, and they were sisters who I still see working around town. One year, my own daughter Rachel and her friend Allison were my PAs. The PAs were not only revered by the little girls but by the leaders as they gave us a chance to take a bathroom break or eat our lunch. Their end-of-camp skit and introduction was the highlight of the closing day.

Every year after my first one had a theme. And I was fortunate to have my partner Debi be Rachel's troop leader and a very experienced scout master. She worked on the badge requirements, so every girl received at least two badges at camp, and I worked on the fun creative stuff. There was the official group name. There was the "chant." Many times during the day, troops would yell out their chant. I still have some of those on my mind, and my daughters still know them all. There were the crafts. We had a specific craft every day to allow the girls to take home something special that they created with the "Craft Ladies." We had our own special craft every day according to our theme. We made a flag for our group. And we made "swaps," which needed to have safety pins attached for swap time on the last day, I loved doing the fun stuff, and Debi loved the badge work.

Over the years, the themes were Under the Sea. And our group was the Sponge Girls. Spice Girls and Sponge Bob were so popular then, I cut up dozens of yellow sponges, and we glued googly eyes on them and made them into Sponge Bob swaps. They were very popular and sought after. One of my favorite crafts was very simple but designed so the girls could shock Mom or Dad in the carpool line. Rubber Beta fish that looked amazingly real were put in a plastic baggie with water. The parents' shocked faces as the girls said, "Look, I got a fish!" were priceless. I don't remember our chant, but the Jelly Fish chant was very memorable. Peanut Butter and Jellyfish, Jellyfish. Hooray for Hollywood was one year. I told Debi everyone will be Starlets or Directors. Let's be the Talent Agents! My chant included, "Don't call us; we'll call you!"

The first day the PAs dressed in gowns and tuxedos, and there were two stretch limos rented, so the parents had to drop off the girls at the park entrance, and the limo would drive them to the shelter entrance. We had a popcorn machine and candy. My last year was The Wild West. I came up with the Pony Express for our group. I sent letters out to famous women and asked for a letter our mail riders could present at the opening ceremony every morning. Guess what? I got then first lady Laura Bush, the NC first lady, soccer sensation Mia Hamm and Secretary of State Hillary Clinton to send letters! All of them said they had been Girl Scouts and were honored to be a part of our Day Camp! Each morning two of our girls would "ride up" on their stick ponies and hand the head leader the mail. The huge surprise the first day with a letter from Laura Bush brought a standing ovation.

It was very hard work but tons of fun. Every evening my daughters and I would come home and get showered, and I would load our sweat-soaked camp shirts into the washer so we would be ready for the next day. The park bathroom was a topic of conversation as we all struggled to pull our sweat-soaked undies up in a sauna-like stall. We had a huge day on Friday when the PAs took over the camp, and they planned the day, and we just followed and laughed. We ate pizza and survived heat and rain, and one time a tornado caused us to seek shelter for 200 girls in a nearby church. So many memories.

Girl Scout Leaders are a special kind of woman and because of the leadership my daughters received over the years is why they stayed in Scouts for the duration. Both of my daughters had the best leaders, and they actually stayed with them throughout their years in their troops. They helped to shape the lives of my daughters and were excellent role models. They were like second mothers to them and taught them and nurtured them, and these ladies devoted countless hours to making this not only an educational experience but a memorable experience as well. Both my girls earned vests covered in badges that meant experiences. They traveled to New York City, on cruises and to camps both local and far away. My favorite weekend trip that I volunteered to chaperone was to the U.S.S. Yorktown in Charleston, SC with Rachel's troop and Miss Debi. We had an excellent time exploring the ship and sleeping in the Junior Officer's quarters. Sean has a very famous experience with her leader Miss Robin. Miss Robin is legendary in our local chapter as being the *only* Daisy leader to take a troop to Carver's Falls. Not even a seasoned veteran leader would take older girls to the dangerous cliffs of Carver's Falls! But Daisy's? That was Sean's first time going camping and away from home without me. She *loved* it! I never ever worried about my girls' security when they were away with their leaders and their troops.

And how about lifelong friendships? Both my daughters have made lasting friendships with their fellow scouts. Both of them are currently roomies with former scouts that they are best friends with. They have been bridesmaids in former scouts' weddings. Every so often, the moms and former leaders do lunch. And whenever I see a cookie booth, I buy, and I say thank you not only to the girls but the mom (or dad) standing in the rain or snow (been there, done that) and I acknowledge them and that they are doing a great job.

So this is my Whisper From The Heart. Memories of friendships, fun, laughter, sticky undies. Time spent with girls and women and girls who have grown into women. Cherish your memories. Cherish the women in your life. Scouts Honor, you will be blessed with these memories.

Chapter

Ten

Shhh, Did You Hear That?
Listen Up
By Debbie Helsel

Debbie Helsel

Debbie is a Heart 2 Heart Healing and Heart 2 Heart Connections Practitioner, additionally trained in Reconnective Healing and Reiki and enjoys working with the energy of crystals. She has a Doctorate of Metaphysical studies through the Alliance of Divine Love Ministry.

Debbie serves as Executive Director at Back to Nature Wildlife Refuge in Orlando, Florida. Since 1990, Debbie has dedicated her life as a federal and state licensed wildlife rehabilitator and public educator, helping to care for Florida's native species wildlife that have been injured or orphaned. In her downtime, she enjoys crystal digging, drum circles, healthy easy listening Christian and Native American music, working in her spiritual garden, bike riding, jogging and anything else that clears the mind and allows messages and inspiration to come through and fill the heart with peace and love.

www.BTNwildlife.org   btndebbie@gmail.com

Shhh, Did You Hear That? Listen Up

By Debbie Helsel

Yep, that's it! That little whispering voice inside that gives you direction and advice when you are in the space of unconditional love, and you stop for a moment to listen and receive those messages and the wisdom that comes along with it.

How do you know when it's "jibber jabber" in your head or a real whisper of wisdom and guidance you are getting? For me, when I am in a quiet space of peace and can truly listen with my whole heart, I hear many guides and angels whispering to me. I believe if you can get into that space, you will know the difference. It is a vulnerable place for me because I am deep into my emotions, and I hear the clearest when I am "in my zone." But I see my vulnerabilities as a positive thing because I am connected to my inner soul and spirit very well, and those whispers from *my* heart have led me down many amazing paths so far in my life, and many more yet to come.

Deep in our hearts, we tuck our wishes and dreams, our fears, our past and present and our future dreams and aspirations. Sometimes we listen and fall to that leap of faith that we are in the right place we are meant to be and to learn the lessons we have come here for. Sometimes it's about being reminded of things like:

You are unique, *you* are worthy, *you* are loved.

You are beautiful, *you* are valued, *you* are loved.

You are healthy, *you* are filled with peace, *you* are loved.

You are generous and kind, *you* are genuine, *you* are loved.

You are the ray of sunshine the world needs, *you* are amazing, *you* are loved.

You share your struggles and vulnerabilities, *you* are so very strong, *you* are loved.

You share your successes and failures, *you* are accepting, *you* are loved.

You share your gifts, *you* are loving, *you* are incredibly special! *You are so very loved!*

Before I got my Doctorate in Metaphysical Studies and Spirituality, I was working on my thesis. When that happened, I started hearing messages very clearly from my guides that were things needing to be talked about and considered. This was the beginning of my "Crystal Garden Adventure Cards," as I called them. It was a lot of information that I was to be sharing and bringing forth at some point in time, but it hasn't happened yet, well, until now. I've never really shared them publically other than with a few people who have been a big part of my spiritual journey.

It all started when I kept hearing words, the same words over and over. The words I kept getting, I also eventually interpreted as symbols. I didn't get it at first why I kept hearing these words, and I just kept trying to dismiss them.

But the words continued to keep coming, almost hounding me until I began writing them down. I had many more questions than I did answers in the beginning. It was just words over and over until I continued to write them down. This went on for weeks, getting 1-3 words a day and sometimes not for days on end, but all without any clue on what I was supposed to do with them. The more I sat in deep meditative reflection with the words (once they stopped coming), I began seeing most of the symbols very clearly in my mind that were to go with each word. I continued writing what I was seeing and hearing but felt there was more to it. It's like having something on the tip of your tongue, and you "know it," but you just cannot get the words out just yet. This went on for weeks, although it felt much longer, feeling like I was being downloaded with tons of information but still given no clear vision or direction on what I was supposed to do with it all. It would even come at random times when I wasn't prepared to write anything down, and I just tried to remember to absorb it the best I could. I decided to just let go and chose to be open and in the moment, in that space of unconditional love and allow spirit to work through me, to come in and to give myself permission to receive the information that was coming.

I knew there was more to this, but I had to allow the time and trust the process so that I was not overwhelmed by it all so consistently. It felt like an exciting adventure that I was on all by myself and felt as if I was supposed to somehow create some kind of help cards. My adventure with the information was the very long process which it took to get from the words out of my head, then onto paper, listen to finally somewhat understand the concept, and move it along to the completion of the process given to me at that time.

I began to see individual bullet-pointed words that kept coming to me about each of the symbols, seemingly to be what I refer to as attributes or other key information related to the symbols. It was as if it was their way to call attention to certain things and thoughts that I would be led to share.

Now, I was like, "Come on now! Really? What the heck is this? It makes no sense to me." But I knew that I was writing down exactly what I was hearing, and since I do not speak the way the words were coming out, I know it was totally divine guidance and messages coming through me as a divine channel or conduit for the information to arrive. I typically work through things in my spiritual garden, which happens to be full of crystals, most of which I went and dug myself, hence the name Crystal Garden Adventure Cards. I talk a bit about how my crystal garden came to be in the collaborative book *When Angels Speak*, also by As You Wish Publishing.

So for months, I randomly received information that was what I would refer to as attributes about each of the words and symbols. I think it came to me slowly so that I was not overwhelmed by the magnitude of the information being shared with me. The attributes were a total surprise as I thought maybe all the objects and symbols' aspects were being shown to me in a different way, kind of like a self-help style. There are things that help us remember who we are and be reminded that we need to "go within" for that true inner knowledge and wisdom, but also that we have help at our disposal, right at our fingertips, and all we have to do is ask for it while being open to the process.

We may "call upon" or "draw upon" certain things, paintings or pictures of things, whether physical or in essence. Spiritual items such as crystals or gem stones are used for assistance in our lives, too, as this seems to be another way to ask for spiritual guidance assistance or help. I feel I was chosen at that time to bring forth the information even though I have yet to share it openly until now.

I am going to share a few of the cards from this current collection (because it feels like more may be coming now!) and explain my interpretation of this information the best I can for you. The information is word-for-word as presented to me. Spirit will be my guide as we choose the ones to share with you here and now. Hopefully, in the near future, I will finish the cards and put them into production, making them available for you to add to your collection.

So, here is how it goes: the card shows a symbol that relates to the initial word I was given, and then the "draw upon" or "call upon" part is next. This means that we can call upon the "energy" or "essence" of an object without actually having to have it there or without being near that object. We use our intuition and can see with our 3rd eye when this happens and are open to it and in the space of unconditional love. In this case, the idea is that we draw upon the energy of the object or whatever your own interpretation of that is for you.

Next to come were the words or attributes I received, and then finally came the explanation of what information or message I was to share. Some symbols have many attributes and messages, while others only have a few, which is why I am not sure this "project" is totally done just yet, and things never fell into place to have them produced just yet.

So, let's start with a Diamond card. So the word "Diamond" came to me, so I wrote it down. The words would come very strongly and boldly to me and would just be a single word at the beginning and nothing else. Then I would hear an attribute, so in this card, the attribute that came was "Temple." This is what I received to go along with this card:

Draw upon or call upon *Diamond* or the *Diamond* symbol for "Temple" (This card has artwork of a diamond shape on it).

"Take your inner and outer temple and surround it with the essence of *Diamond*. Draw *Diamond* around you, above and below you and its sheer strength and stability will protect you from the unknown or the unwelcome sources that will try to influence you in ways that may not be of the divine light."

Let's look at another. Being mindful here that I am sharing the ones that my "whispers" from deep inside my heart are asking me to share at this time. So, whoever they are meant for, you're welcome!

Draw upon or call upon *Fire* or the *Fire* symbol for "Restructure" (This card has artwork depicting a phoenix rising from fire).

"*Fire* will help you restructure yourself on the inside and out. Call upon *Fire* to help burn away the unnecessary and allow opportunities to emerge anew in whatever areas in your life that need a shift."

Draw upon or call upon *Moon* or the *Moon* symbol for "Radiance" (This card has artwork depicting a crescent moon laying back, resting on a swirl with stars).

"*Moon* will fill us with such radiance; we need to accept the radiance it sheds and shares and project it out even further from ourselves. Seeing past the "now" that is now. Just as seasons change and our moods change, so does the change occur for the *Moon*. *Moon* reminds us to be loving and knows that there is always change for and to everything."

Draw upon or call upon *Mountain* or the *Mountain* symbol for "Solitude" (This card has artwork depicting three mountain peaks, one in front and 1 behind each side).

"When *Mountain* shows us the time of need that is of being alone, just you and *Mountain*, *Mountain* will help you balance and find the aspects of self that might be tucked away at the moment."

Draw upon or call upon *Star* or the *Star* symbol for "Light" (This card has artwork of a star with little stars on a swirl that is fanciful).

"*Star* will be that spark of light you need when it seems like everything around you is falling apart, and you can't seem to stop it. It will illuminate a path for you if you stop and just pay attention to the light *Star* is trying to bestow upon you. It will rejuvenate you when you are feeling tired and run down, giving you peace and a way to let go of that which does not suit you. It will brighten even your darkest times. Open your heart to *Star* and let it light the way."

Draw upon or call upon *Tree* or the *Tree* symbol for "Knowledge" (This artwork has a tree with hearts as the leaves).

"Tree has a knowing that most don't even consider. *Tree* is an elder one and should be regarded as such and should be highly respected at all times. Be sure you are respecting those with greater knowledge and learn from them."

All of the cards have more than one attribute that have been offered. *Tree* has some powerful cards, so here is another from *Tree*.

Draw upon or call upon *Tree* or the *Tree* symbol for "Tranquility" (This artwork is the same design as the other tree card).

"Spend some time admiring *Tree*. Notice *Tree*'s size, shape, height, and color. Know that *Tree* is a gift from the Creator, a piece of beauty, one of a kind, just like us."

Draw upon or call upon *Flower* or the *Flower* symbol for "Growth and Change" (This artwork is a stemmed flower that is almost like a lotus flower).

"*Flower* shows you beauty and change, just as *Flower* blooms and spreads its petals, so you do as well, spreading the petals of your life and blossom. Though the *Flower* blossoms or blooms may only last a short time, it stimulates growth and a beginning to which there is no end. Only the boundaries we place on it."

So as I share some of these intuitive cards that came to me, I feel that there was purpose in the fact that I was led to share them with you. I hope that the specific cards I included here may have spoken to each of you in some way or at least gave you a moment in time to ponder the message that was presented and subject to your own interpretation of the information.

In our fast-moving world these days, I pray that we can all love each other as one, learn to be kind to one another, showing compassion and respect for each other and meeting each other halfway on our journeys, and moving forward together in growth and in the space of unconditional love and acceptance.

I believe we are all here to learn, teach and grow together and that we all have messages that we are here to share with each other. Hopefully, our "direct connect"conduits stay clear and open, keeping us as the clear and perfect channels from the Divine source that we are. We are the keepers of this planet and of each other. Our everyday decisions have an effect on the outcome for our futures, and I pray that we are mindful of our actions and learn how we can all do a little better to care for one another and for this amazing planet we live on. Be blessed.

I would like to dedicate this segment to honor my longtime mentor and dear friend Vicki High. Vicki was an amazing soul that touched my life in more ways than I can count. She challenged me to really dig in and think about things in new ways and to get to the core of things, and work to love unconditionally while learning to let go of the things that no longer served my life. Vicki was so full of life and inspiration, wanting only to share her gifts with the world. Her love was the most giving and caring, although her driving was a little strong. She was one of the greatest people I have ever met in my life, and I am exceptionally blessed to have been a part of her life. She loved me when I felt unlovable and held me up during my deepest pains. She walked beside me through the greatest trials of my life so far and never waivered in her love and support even once. I owe a great deal of my spiritual growth to Vicki. My life will not be the same without her, but I know she's never far away and is always tucked inside, sharing with whispers from my heart.

Chapter

Eleven

Speak Up, I Can't Hear You
By Patricia Holgate Haney

Patricia Holgate Haney

Inspired by her love of books passed down by her father, she immersed herself in the written word and dreamed of exploring the world.

After careers in both the for-profit and non-profit world, her passion for travel, as well as writing, continue to expand. She has been published in three compilation books, *Love Meets Life*, *Ordinary Oneness* and *Wisdom of the Silver Sisters, Guiding Grace.*

She and her husband Gary enjoy travel, cooking and spending time with their family, which includes two sons, three grandchildren and three great-grandchildren. She volunteers for organizations that are dedicated to helping the underserved and ensuring equality for all.

You can reach her by e-mail at whispers@phtravels.com

Her website is: phtravels.com

https://www.amazon.com/author/patriciaholgatehaney

Speak Up, I Can't Hear You
By Patricia Holgate Haney

I can still hear my Dad's response when my siblings or I responded to my father by saying, "Huh?" when we didn't listen. It was, "Huh, hell, listen and learn something." That resonates in a whole different way today.

I am sure I am not alone in being caught in the middle of the argument between "good and bad," or as depicted in cartoons where the devil sits on one shoulder and the angel on the other, both whispering in our ear the reason we should do what they say.

I have always believed that there are few things that are one hundred percent good or bad. As we go through life, experiences add to our decision-making, and we learn to weigh the information we have with the actual circumstances and find that there are times when "grey" is more accurate instead of being good or bad or black and white.

When I was young, my parents were the ones who identified what good or acceptable behavior was. I learned that life was easier to live within their rules and had no reason to question or challenge them, even if I didn't want to eat the broccoli!

Growing up, we become exposed to more "voices": teachers, neighbors, friends, religious leaders, media, and more. At times, there was a cacophony of voices too loud to whisper, more like a high decibel rock concert.

My paternal "Grams" always had new sayings, almost as many as the recipes she collected. She posted some of them in the numerous spiral index card collections she had handwritten with much detail, including personal notes sharing her thoughts about different entries. She had also collected and cut out, and pasted quotes, recipes and newspaper columns. Grams titled her little booklets, *Gleanings from Grams.* She enjoyed sharing what she had learned with others, and she told me that it gave her much joy to do so. I came across one of those books recently and enjoyed reading through it again. It felt as if she were sharing her "whispers." Reading it brought a smile to my heart, and I felt her presence.

A couple of quotes she shared were:

"Write in your heart that every day is the best day of the year." —Ralph Waldo Emerson

"Shoot for the moon. Even if you miss, you'll land among the stars." —Norman Vincent Peale

I seemed to have the knack for conversations; no one stayed a stranger long. I was always curious about other people and their experiences and outlook. I learned new things and found myself excited to try them myself and explore the world.

While I may have been good at listening to others, I did not listen to myself.

At times, there would be a faint whisper, and other times it was a booming voice. Both versions could be positive or negative, but as many of us tend to do, I seemed to listen to the negative, picky, critical voices. My gut or instinct may have told me otherwise, but I ignored those and paid attention when I heard the whispers saying, you're not good enough, pretty, intelligent, talented, instead of the voices trying to grab my attention and telling me, you rock, you did it, you can do it.

Maybe at some point, my intense interest in religion and the bible, which began at an early age, left me with the misconception that thinking of myself in a positive manner meant I was too prideful, not humble enough. That can be the problem with being too young to think critically about what you are reading or being told.

One of the many reasons I didn't care for the kids' programs at church was because everything seemed superficial as far as exploring the meanings and applying them to life – with maybe the exception of the ten commandments.

I was fortunate that Grams had a strong sense of faith, but it was not exclusionary. I was able to look to her as an example. She relied on her faith for strength through trying times but also to express gratitude.

She had a sense of humor that made anything more fun. She emphasized that we all make mistakes, and it is what we do afterward that counts. She always made me feel that

I could do anything and that both she and Gramps and God would be there for me. I always wished she had lived closer because I adored spending time with them both.

Growing up in the 50s and 60s provided a lot of contrasts in right and wrong. It was an age where generations began to question the status quo loudly. With more voices to sift through, why did my voice take the back seat?

I jumped right into the fray of change. I used my voice by speaking up in public, writing personal letters in various campaigns, feeling like I was making my voice heard for good. My participation was a great experience, but I spent a lot of time on what I'll call my public voice vs. listening to my inner whispers.

They say hindsight is always 20/20, and I think it is indeed true. Time after time, my inner voice whispered to me, and I tended to shut it down. I was always concerned about what other people might think I should do or be, but how crazy is that?

On my shoulders, the annoying devil and angel were joined by my whispers, my gut feelings, and my heart. I locked them away in the same vault and tried to ignore them all.

I knew the answers; I refused to trust myself and my voice.

The whispers could have been about relationships, finances, children, pretty much anything. I was so focused on societal and my peers' ideas of what was right and what I perceived as irreconcilable failures that I muffled those whispers.

Maybe this was supposed to happen. Perhaps with the experience gained while not listening to my inner voice, I was better able to appreciate it and give it the value it deserved when I finally did.

Time and thoughtful meditation have helped me realize that whispers are the soft voices you *sense* as much as you feel. My instincts have been developed by reactions to what I have experienced in my subconscious.

Intuition is gained through direct knowledge or being cognizant without rational thought and inference. All these voices and feelings evolve and change based on experiences, that which has happened, and experiences and paying attention and seeing.

I look back and can see or maybe imagine what might have been, but I had a wonderful friend who recently passed named Joan who always said, "it is what it is, it was what it was, it will be what it will be."

Now some people may take that quote or belief as resignation; I take it as a potential possibility.

I am still a work in progress. Learning to accept the past, using it to grow personally, and make tomorrow as brilliant as I can. No, I'm not a Pollyanna. I am choosing to believe that if I put out positive vibes, actions, and words, karma is kinder. I feel that gratitude and kindness beget the same.

Will it always be a happy sunshiny day? No, but I can deal with potholes and roadblocks in my life journey because I truly believe my future holds better days.

I know that my heart plays into my voice as well. The common opinion is that our heart reflects our innermost character or inclination and courage as much as it does love. Your heart not only keeps your blood pumping; it holds your inner whispers or voices in its vault. I am learning not to lock them up tight and instead let my whispers reside and become nourished there.

I used to journal in tough times only. It was a way to keep track of my feelings and events. As time went on, I began journaling every day and found it to be a great way to connect my feelings and use them as a reference.

Our inner voices can be full of love and encouragement. Mine had even guided and encouraged me when I documented my experiences and feelings through the most challenging and darkest times. I have doubted myself, but journaling helped me believe in my inner voice, my whisper.

I am trying to get better at meditation. I am learning that it is ok to have quiet time every day and embrace the solitude. I hear my whispers more clearly. Journaling afterward helps me realize what power I do have. It helps direct me and ground me.

One other thing I've learned is that I need to listen to the whisper for understanding. I've got it wrong so many times. Shocking, I know!

Re-evaluating, I think that I heard what I wanted to hear. Maybe it was easier that way at the time, but the easy way is not always the best. We must respect our truth and be true to ourselves the same as we must be to others.

Falling in love with a narcissist was easy. On the surface, charming and bright. Below the surface, scheming, manipulative, they love to prove their superiority by demeaning everyone else. As someone told me once, "he would sell his mother out to get what he wants, and she wouldn't see it coming." I share this part of my story for anyone who has similar whispers, gut feelings, whatever, pay attention. You are not alone, and you will do yourself a favor by getting out of the situation as fast as you can. It wasn't easy for me.

I know I'm not the only one who has been in a relationship where the whispers were telling me that it was a mistake. I wanted, maybe I needed, it to work, or perhaps I was lonely and not content enough to be alone or, worse yet, afraid to admit I made or was making a mistake. I was going into the relationship and not listening to my gut. This became costly emotionally. Toss in the guilt I felt because I had also involved everyone else in my family, I found myself crippled by guilt, shame, failure, lack of self-esteem, and confidence. Good Lord, in hindsight, it was ridiculous.

I found myself living a lie. I told myself I did it because I believed I could fix it. I was afraid to be a failure again. My inner voice kept whispering and then shouting, "it's not working; you are losing yourself!"

Eventually, I sought out a therapist who helped me realize what was happening. I was able to shake off the feeling and belief that I was crazy. I learned to make the changes I needed and take my instincts seriously. I had fallen into the proverbial rabbit hole.

I fell in, but I climbed out. I kept beating myself up for a while feeling that I should have known what was happening, but I began to focus instead on the fact that I made it out. In short, your voice speaks, but you must listen, and I didn't. I learned the lesson the hard way, but I did understand.

Journaling helps to identify what you are feeling and your problem, and reading it back is healing. Another area where this has been beneficial is health-wise.

As a woman, I also realized that I need to listen to my inner voice regarding physical well-being. It is hard when you go to seek help from a doctor and you are not in the "demographic" of certain conditions. They may dismiss or gaslight you by blowing off the symptoms you know you are feeling, trying to convince you that you imagine them.

For years, I went through a series of events that eventually almost resulted in my death. Only by being persistent was I able to make it out of this near-death experience and fortunately find doctors who trusted my instinct that "something is not right." My journal entries were extremely helpful in this area.

Do you listen to your voice? Do you let others overrule your gut feeling?

There are times where your inner voice must poke you *hard* to help you hear what it is trying to say or tell you. I know it happened to me more than once. Unexpected, not on my radar.

While working for a year on a remote job assignment, I was part of a team from across the nation recruited to work on a significant project. Strangers who became a core group of peers and then life-long friends.

One of the team members was Gary. We began to forge a real friendship. I was older, divorced, and not looking for a relationship. Gary had never been married. Maybe that helped.

We used to get comments that "you guys have so much in common." The commonality I saw was that we were both family-oriented, loved travel, loved to read and cook and laugh. I was more spontaneous; he was more conservative.

Our core workgroup worked long hours, but still managed under stressful situations, to have fun and share a lot of laughter. Some or all of us took weekend road trips to various destinations. At one point, we saw a major sale on airfare to Europe. None of the others were interested.

Gary and I planned a trip with his cousin and my youngest son to Europe. We had a great time exploring new places and experiences. We found that we traveled well together, which is always a good test for relationships. We all got along and made plans for future trips.

"There is something here," said my inner voice, but I shut it down. Nope, no way. Not because of him, but because of me. I didn't want to spoil a great friendship with a serious relationship.

For over three years, we had a long-distance relationship, and it began to get serious. My inner voice was no longer whispering. It was shaking me by the shoulders and saying, "C'mon, girl, he is the one." I began to listen closely and believe. He gave me my engagement ring almost 25 years ago, on the fourth of July. We got married that October and have never looked back.

I guess the moral of this part of my story is that not listening to your whispers can not only result in finding yourself in a negative situation, but you may miss the potential for positivity. Whether it is love, career, finance, any segment of life. I would have missed out on the glorious years I have had if I had not finally listened.

Why are we more open to hearing the negative than the positive? I feel that it has to do with our self-awareness. I began to take time daily to revel in silence, listen to my inner whispers, express gratitude, and journal. I found ways to give back in appreciation, and I have genuinely felt better for it. My life began to change for the positive in all areas.

I was more receptive, more aware, and more in touch with my spirituality. You can do it too. Your inner voice or whisper can help guide you through life on all levels. Remember, though, that your life experiences also have a play in this. If you have trouble listening to your voice, meditate, journal, and seek help if needed.

Going back to my bible studies, Proverbs 4:6-7 says, "Do not forsake wisdom, and she will protect you, love her, and she will watch over you. Wisdom is supreme, therefore get wisdom."

Now I better understand that wisdom is not always the same as understanding. Wisdom is an element of character, where understanding is a process of comprehension that is more mental and is subjective.

I believe both are integral parts of the formula to help you transcribe your whispers.

I had this gem written inside the cover of one of my journals.

The Voice

There is a voice inside of you

That whispers all day long

"I feel that this is right for me,

I know that this is wrong."

No teacher, preacher, parent, friend

or wise man can decide

What's right for you – just listen to

The voice that speaks inside."

—Shel Silverstein

We all share the ability to hear our whispers; we need to take the time to acknowledge and *trust* the message.

Let's work on helping each other hear and listen and trust.

Chapter

Twelve

Undivided: Four Strategies to
go from Fear to Peace
By Donna Kiel

Donna Kiel

Donna Kiel is a life coach, healer, teacher, leader, university professor, and a guide for those seeking a life free of suffering and one that is joyful. Donna has a unique ability to inspire you to discover and live your highest potential. Donna's expertise, training, and her engaging and welcoming style provide the compassion and connection needed to discover your own genius and passion. Donna takes people from darkness to light and is a woman who works for equity and empathy in every context. Donna holds a doctorate in educational leadership and is a certified counselor and certified Martha Beck Wayfinder life coach. Donna created the empathy framework with practical tools to lead individuals and organizations to experience new levels of connection, creativity, and success. Donna is often sought for innovative change efforts by organizations and individuals seeking solutions to systemic and life challenges. Donna inspires, enlivens, and creates useful and practical solutions. Donna is the epitome of inspiration and integrity for those seeking meaning, insight, and concrete answers to the next steps in life. Donna is currently a professor, speaker, coach, and mentor offering workshops, individual coaching, anxiety relief, career planning, and life mapping sessions.

She can be reached at drdonnakiel@gmail.com or through her website at https://donnakiel.com.

Undivided: Four Strategies to go from Fear to Peace

By Donna Kiel

What is troubling you right now? What, if you could, would you change about your life? What is whispering to you to change so that you can be more of yourself? For decades of my life, I had convinced myself that I knew those things in my life I wanted to change. I knew I wanted to write, coach, and have a positive impact. I knew I wanted to change the pace of my life, the long work hours, and my constant busyness each day. I could feel a tug to spend more time with me. I thought I could hear the whispers telling me to have more self-care. Each day, I would write in my journal how I planned to take care of myself, spend time writing, and practice self-care. And each day, I would jump into work and quiet the whispers saying I would like to write, but I'm afraid someone will get mad, or I'm afraid the work I get paid for won't get done. I was always one big bundle of people-pleasing fear.

Along with people-pleasing and being a big introvert, I am an approval addict. Before the pandemic, I had a daily schedule that consisted of working 12 hours a day, coming home, and doing emails until falling asleep with my laptop in my lap. My emails were filled with people thanking me for the work I had done for them and with endless requests for more work. It seemed the more efficient I was in answering emails, doing more for people, and meeting their needs, the more requests I had for work. I never seemed to catch up. I would wake up and immediately get on my email to attempt to get ahead of the list. I never could get ahead. I never found that time I wanted to write. I never did the self-care I promised myself each day. I numbed the feelings of regret, anger, of disappointment in myself with work and with scrolling social media and with making more to-do lists. I had become divided from my truth and lost within my rituals of lies to myself.

Then, in March of 2020, the global pandemic offered me a free ticket to my dreams. I was elated to have a lockdown order. An introvert, I now had my dream come true of being told I had to stay home, away from people, and to isolate. I convinced my little introverted self that isolation was bliss. I locked away, just like the rest of the world, with my little pod of people and my rescue dog Gracie. Gracie, like me, is very introverted and anxious. She doesn't like change, is not too fond of people, except for me, and likes to be alone. We are perfect for each other. I now could finally listen to the whispers telling me to take care of myself and to write, to create the life I dreamed of, and to be true to my feelings, wants, and dreams. It was just one day into the pandemic when that all fell apart.

On the first day of the pandemic lockdown, I listened to news reports of people losing jobs and organizations shutting down. Panic hit me like a tidal wave washing away any hope of kicking back and making time for me. What I do when I panic is very interesting. I kick into an overdrive of creativity. That first day I began emailing ideas of how I could help schools with remote teaching and help teachers to figure out this new modality. I emailed my bosses with ideas for new programs and potential new revenue. I was on a creativity blitz. I worked 20 hours a day creating and hyperventilating about how to make myself indispensable. If I lost my work identity, I would lose myself. On day one of the pandemic, I discovered that there was no "me" without work. So, I hunkered down, my rescue dog and me and worked, and worked and worked. And so, for the 14 months of the pandemic, I lost who I was to work. It took 14 months to hear the whisper that would bring me back to myself. The journey of those 14 months was the most painful, joyful, confusing, and enlightening moment of my life. Along that way, I found four practical steps to shed the fear and welcome ease.

Step One – Get Angry

For those of us who are lost in the trap of needing the validation of others to show ourselves we matter, anger is something we stuff away and fear. We can't possibly get mad when we deny ourselves what we want or when others ask us to put them first because we would risk not getting the approval we crave and need. For me, I am deathly afraid of anger. Anger feels uncontrollable and unpredictable.

Throughout the pandemic, every so often, when wearing a mask, I would feel this tingling by my lips. I dismissed the feeling because I was way too busy to notice. The feeling was a whisper. Then, after 14 months of lockdown, a friend asked me to make plans for a vacation. I couldn't imagine going on a vacation. I had work to do. But I knew vacation planning would make her happy. Then it happened. The whisper became a shout. As my friend pushed me for dates for a vacation, the anger surged inside me. I snapped. I said I had to go to the doctor to check out this tingling in my lips, so I can't go on vacation until that is taken care of. I don't even know where that thought came from. I hadn't thought of going to the doctor before I shouted it at her. It was as if someone took the lid of the anger and fear all at the same time.

Anger is often the gatekeeper of truth. If we can allow ourselves the safety to feel angry. If we can voice our anger with care and truth, the anger may open the doors so that we can hear the whisper. What about your life gets you angry right now? Who pushes your buttons? Write down all those things you are angry at. Within those things may be an important whisper – it was for me.

Step Two – Stop

Anger opens a door that can easily be shut again if we don't stop, pause, and allow truth to take hold. The "stop" is truly the most important thing we can do. In a world that is constantly moving with social media sharing what we should be doing and should be wanting, it is so easy to never stop, never notice, and ignore what we want and need. Anger can also be so frightening that we spew the anger away in an attempt to gather control. Instead, allow the anger and then stop. Pause to ask, "Why?"

I had to figure out why I was so angry that my friend wanted to go on vacation. It took a while, but I realized that was the breaking point. She was taking care of herself. Her taking care of herself had put the spotlight on the reality that for 14 months of a pandemic, I had ignored myself. I had ignored my health, my happiness, and my relationships. I had adopted the personality of my rescue dog Gracie. I was a good little worker, just as Gracie barks at the Amazon deliveries. I had shunned all people in my life just as Gracie runs away from anyone who comes near her. I had lost who I wanted to be, who I dreamed of being. I had moved so fast that life was passing by me.

When I stopped, rather than ask why I was angry, I had to ask myself, what do I need to stop? I realized that I didn't want to go on vacation because I didn't want the pause in work. I wanted to stop work. I wanted to stop and to start. If you feel angry and if you find that you are denying what you want and saying "but I have to" each day, then stop. Ask yourself what you need to stop doing.

Once I stopped, life's whisper got louder. A virtual doctor visit and then hospital ER visit revealed a parotid tumor as the cause of the sensation in my lips. My body had taken over where my mind had failed me. I had lost myself to people-pleasing, to work identity, and to promises of dreams that would be realized tomorrow with tomorrow never coming. Fear had consumed my integrity and divided me from my truth.

Step Three – Cave into Fear

Our culture often tells us to think positive, be joyful, find gratitude and deny those feelings that are dark and fearful. Denying our fear and anxiousness just allows those feelings to fester in the darkness creating monsters that become larger than life when released. But if we can cave into fear, allowing it to wash over us, and listening to the whispers of the fear guiding us, then we can align with our integrity and grow closer to our true self.

For me, the diagnosis of a tumor was like a match thrown on gasoline of fear. The explosion of anxiety rocked everything in my world. I wish I could say that I dared to just allow the fear to be and witness it. The truth is I had no choice. The fear consumed me, and I couldn't shake it. I had to find a way to face that fear and name it. I started writing a letter to God each morning, in the quiet. The quiet was new for me. I typically turn on the TV or some noise the moment I wake. I fill the air with anything to distract from painful feelings. Now, the fear was too much. In the letter, I would pour my heart out to God, asking for help, grasping for hope, and sharing each moment of anxiety. I would then pause and meditate, and God would write me back. The messages were the part of me that is still and knows the truth of God in my life. Only by caving in to the fear could I access the truth of my connection to God that would allow me to know that God has given me, and all of us, everything we need to be in this life. Of course, God would tell me of the love God has for me and of the love that heals and will set me free.

Step Four – Choose

Healing the division of our lives that results from doing and saying things we do not want to say or do requires humility. We have such pride and arrogance thinking that we know why we are people-pleasing and working so hard. We believe we know better – at least I thought I did. I thought I had to say yes when I wanted to say no so that I could keep a job and continue to get a paycheck. I thought I knew what was best for making everyone happy so that I could avoid conflict. What I was avoiding was living my truth and what I was choosing was suffering.

During the time of diagnosis, biopsies, and awaiting surgery, I was consumed by fear. I had thought I was consumed by fear of death, fear of illness, and fear of the unknown, but what I came to realize is that my real fear was the fear of how I was living my life and that I wouldn't ever choose me and create an undivided life. In one of my letters from God, God wrote to me of the choices I have made. I had chosen fear of rejection, fear of abandonment, fear of anger when I could have chosen my truth instead. I didn't want to please others. I didn't want to work so hard. I wanted to write, to create, to play. While I had chosen the fear of abandonment, rejection, and anger, I had chosen to abandon myself, reject my own needs and wants, and treat myself with anger.

A friend asked me if I truly can sit in the joy that is in my life. She asked if after I meditate or write my letters to God if I sit in that moment and allow the feeling of joy. If I pause and choose me and choose what I want and what I need to feel ease. I didn't. I had made my own anger, stopping, and caving into fear as another task to do. Now, instead of distracting with work, I was distracting from my truth with fear and fixes. Just that one question: could I sit with joy and let it wash over me? That one question shifted me and allowed the whisper to be clear. Do you allow joy to permeate your being and to embrace the fear and the ease? Each time my heart aches and I feel a tug, I know my soul is whispering to me to find what I am angry about, to stop, to cave into fear, and to choose me.

Allowing the whisper to speak your truth is a life-changing and transformational experience. It took me most of my life to listen to the whisper. Working hard to avoid fear had silenced the sound of my truth and had allowed me to deny the ease that we all deserve – that I deserved. The moment I stopped avoiding fear and instead allowed fear of death, fear of changing who I am, and fear of the truth of my own joy to wash over me, I could step into ease and peace. You deserve to feel peace each day of your life. You deserve to allow fear, allow pain, allow sorrow, for it is in the allowing of all of those challenging feelings that we can finally also allow the joy and happiness of a life of truth and peace.

Chapter

Thirteen

Hold On: You Are
Not Done Here
By Amy I. King

Amy I. King

Amy I King is a Certified Life Coach and owner of Your Phenomenal Life, LLC. She taught in public education for a decade before returning to school for her coaching certification. She is a contributing author of international bestsellers: *Inspirations: 101 Uplifting Stories for Daily Happiness, Manifestations: True Stories of Bringing the Imagined into Reality, and The Grateful Soul: The Art and Practice of Gratitude*, among others.

Amy enjoys spending time with friends, listening to great music of a variety of genres, reading, writing, and adventure. She enjoys travel both solo and with loved ones. She loves meeting new people and making new connections.

Amy has overcome a plethora of challenges that make her the woman she is today. She was born with Spina bifida, which now requires her to use a wheelchair. Despite the many challenges she has faced, she has created a life that is filled with wonderful people who have helped her create amazing memories. She has most recently overcome breast cancer. Every challenge, Amy believes, is put before us to help us to evolve and grow into the greatest version of ourselves.

Amy's greatest joy is using her personal experiences and wisdom to help others move past their personal blocks and outdated beliefs to become empowered to live the life of their dreams.

She loves developing relationships with her clients built on trust and vulnerability. She focuses on coaching teens and women. She is currently coaching and working on her first solo book, *Messy Wheels: Stories from Where I Sit*, available on Amazon in 2022. She can be reached at (916) 718-0914. She welcomes the opportunity to work with you to help you build the life of your dreams.

Hold On: You Are Not Done Here

By Amy I. King

"If I had to use a wheelchair, I would kill myself." The words came out of her mouth and slapped me across the face as I sat with a group of women, socializing. It stung as if a million bees had hit me all at once. I usually put my emotional armor on but hadn't that day as I thought, "You won't need it; they are your friends." Many years ago, there was a time at the beginning of my journey as a wheelchair user when I felt exactly as she does.

I had recently graduated college with a degree in History and had an excellent job working in the computer software industry. I had been promoted quickly from a brand new tester with zero computer software testing experience to a Quality Assurance Lead. A group of five to seven testers was under my supervision for each project. The job and the people with whom I worked were incredible. A family formed in our department. We were a rowdy bunch, meeting on Friday evenings at the local watering hole to decompress, connect, and have fun. I was having the time of my life. Then the rug was pulled out from under me.

Forearm crutches were what I had used for years, having been born with Spina bifida. My gait suddenly began to change. When I would swing my legs through, upon landing, my right hip jutted out. This was not normal; something was wrong.

A doctor determined that I had a herniated disk and began the protocol. It became more and more laborious to walk, and I was experiencing excruciating pain. Eventually, I had to get a wheelchair for work. I left the wheelchair with security in the afternoons. They would roll it out to my car in the morning, and I would use it for the day. At the time, the home I lived in was a split level. I did a lot of what I call scooting. I would be on my butt, legs in front of me, and using my arms to scoot me across the floor to get around the house. Not something I would recommend, as it eventually caused a pressure wound to develop.

At the same time that all of this was happening, one of my supervisors was leaving the company and wanted me to go with her. There had been so many lay-offs that it seemed inevitable I would eventually be on the chopping block. I interviewed with her new boss and was offered a job and a substantial salary increase. I accepted the offer and gave notice. The company I was with countered the proposal with more money. I stayed for the money. A few months later, I was laid-off. I cleared my personal belongings, said goodbye to my co-workers, and left. I went home knowing that looking for another job was out of the question, for now. In hindsight, I wish I had taken the position at the other company, but we live and learn.

Day after day, I spent alone, becoming more and more depressed. For pain, I had been given Vicodin, and at that time, safeguards weren't in place to protect patients from addiction. So my prescription was filled whenever I needed it.

There were many times when I felt so depressed, alone, sad, at the end of my rope, in such a dark hole that I just wanted it all to end. Day in and day out, I felt lost and completely alone. I realized that if I just took all of the Vicodin, it would be over. Night after night, I lined the Vicodin up and thought I would be free if I just took a massive handful of pills. Finally, there was one particular night when I was completely done. I hadn't had any friends visit or call, and I felt like life was never going to get better. I had gone from having an excellent job, lots of socialization with the people I worked with, and friends I had outside of work, not to mention dating. Now I spent my days doing absolutely nothing but checking out chat rooms, trying to find some support.

I lined the Vicodin up, ready to end it all. Then, I heard it. "Don't do it. Be patient. You are not finished here." I looked around as if I would see someone. But, again, I heard the voice. "You have more to do. Don't do it." Crying, I shoved all of the pills back into the bottle. At that point, I decided to have faith in that voice, be patient, and see what life had in store.

I was depressed, lonely, feeling trapped in a split-level home, driving a vehicle that I had proudly purchased only a few months prior. Now, I would have to trade in for something that could give me a bit more independence. A different wheelchair was also required, as lifting a 50 lb. wheelchair just wasn't feasible. This was in the earlier days of the Internet. There were chat rooms for all different topics of conversation. I found refuge in the chat rooms and support from others who were experiencing similar situations.

In the Spring, about 5 months after I was laid off, my mom and I were invited to a friend's wedding in Germany. We decided to go and to add Berlin and Paris to our trip. We had friends in Belgium who would meet us in Paris. We learned a lot about traveling in a wheelchair. I was brought to the plane door in something resembling a cherry picker. We attended our friend's wedding in Germany with help getting me up the stairs of the ancient church. It was an all-day and all-night affair. Fantastic food, dancing, and of course the release of 99 red balloons with messages of good wishes. After a few days with our friends, we were off to Berlin. There, we were staying at a bed and breakfast. When we arrived, we realized that my wheelchair was not going to fit through the front door. So, the man of the house, Lars, took it upon himself to become a wheelchair mechanic. He took apart the chair to change the wheels' camber so that it would be narrow enough to fit through the narrow doors. It was quite the adventure. We saw all of Berlin and were off to Paris, arguably the most beautiful city in the world.

I fell in love with the architecture of the city. It gave me goosebumps thinking about the history and all of the people who had been there. At the Louvre, I was brought to tears in front of the Mona Lisa. History had been my major, and I was geeking out big time! Next, we visited the Picasso museum, which houses works from each of his periods. Sacre cour and Notre dam were incredible, and to think I would have missed all of this if I had taken those pills. Life, I realized, was so worth living. I had just been living in a very limiting situation, and that needed to change.

When we returned, I finally saw a neurosurgeon who knew right away what was wrong. Correctly diagnosed with a tethered spinal cord, I had surgery to relieve the pain and prevent further damage.

I moved back to the Sacramento valley, where I had been raised. I rented an apartment that was completely wheelchair accessible, traded my car in for something that I could get in and out of, and was finally approved for a lighter-weight wheelchair. I was regaining my independence in a completely new way.

I found a job working as a revenue analyst. After having decided to continue my education, I began taking credentialing classes to become a teacher. When I first started my History degree, becoming a teacher was my intention, but I had been sidetracked by the computer software industry.

One night, watching the news, a report showed people living with physical challenges playing hockey in sleds at the local ice rink. That looked like fun! I was strong from almost 30 years on forearm crutches but had never participated in sports and had been exempt from P.E. classes in school. Now, in my early thirties, I was thinking about playing hockey! After trying it out, I was hooked! The freedom I felt gliding across the ice was glorious. I ordered a custom sled, purchased a helmet and all of the protective padding. You might be wondering about the logistics. A person sits in a bucket seat attached to a sled with their legs straight out in front of them. They are strapped into the bucket. Two blades are underneath the bucket.

You propel yourself forward by using two short hockey sticks with blades on the ends, one in each hand the hockey player glides across the ice. This was the first time since I was four years old that I had been with other people with physical challenges. I was raised in a family where I was not labeled as disabled or exposed to other people with physical challenges. I was mainstreamed in school after two years at a preschool that catered to children with physical challenges. There, I learned how to climb stairs, get in and out of a bathtub independently, and gain the physical strength I needed to use crutches. I didn't have the identity of disabled when I was walking on forearm crutches. It was a bit of an adjustment, to be honest. We practiced every Saturday morning at the local ice rink. It was fun, exercise, and I felt empowered, strong, a part of something. I also began training for the Susan G. Komen Race for the Cure. I had a goal to roll that 5k in 32 minutes which would be a consistent 10-minute mile. I trained daily, rolling up and down hills and streets. On the day of the race, I finished in 32 minutes 26 seconds. I was so proud and filled with joy! I was feeling a freedom that using crutches had never afforded me.

After I finished my credentialing program, I began teaching in a Title I high school in the district where I had been hoping I would be hired. My students taught me more than I could have ever taught them. They taught me that people who don't have a lot share a lot. They taught me that people are people and that there is worth in every person, including someone who happens to use a wheelchair. I don't think that using a wheelchair was ever an issue for my students past the first day when I would tell students why. After that, it was business as usual with so many volunteer helpers, I never had to worry about anything. One of the funniest things that have ever happened due to my wheelchair use was on that campus. I was attending a staff meeting. I had become close to a colleague who started at the school at the same time. We had been sitting together. When the meeting adjourned, I backed up, caught a table leg with my big wheel, and flipped backward. The principal looked at my friend and asked, "Does that happen a lot?" Thankfully, it doesn't happen a lot. Wheelchair users know the center of gravity on their chairs. The only other time that had happened was on a dance floor. But, what can I say? Sometimes that twirl goes wrong!

Of course, there have been many challenges in using a wheelchair. My teacher friend and I decided to travel to Kauai one Christmas vacation for a week. We got there, and it poured day and night. We made some calls and decided to move to Oahu for the remainder of our vacation. I had called the hotel directly and told them that I needed a wheelchair-accessible room. We get to the hotel, are taken to our room, and guess what!? It was not wheelchair accessible. I couldn't even get my wheelchair through the bathroom door. Now what?! I was having a meltdown. The manager brought me a tin of cookies. I looked at her and said, "How are cookies supposed to help me get into the bathroom?" I was losing it! I got it together, and we started calling other hotels. Finally, we found a room on the beach that would be more expensive but worth having an accessible bathroom. We ended up having a great time for the remainder of our trip.

I bought my first house and, with my basset hound Lucy made it my home. Life was good, and I was happy, thriving, and independent.

There have been countless good things that have come out of the past 20 years since I became a wheelchair user. Hockey brought me to waterskiing. I had never felt so free in my life than when I was on that water! I began entering wake crossing competitions, often taking first place. My inner athlete had emerged. Thriving and happy, I began dating and socializing with new friends. Yet, when I think about what I would have missed out on, it devastates me. I sometimes cry for that woman who felt so alone and so isolated.

Again, I reflected on life and realized that I would have missed out on so much if I hadn't held on. I think of all of the beautiful memories that have been made over the past 20 years. Holding my nephew for the first time and whispering to him that I would always love him no matter what, getting a second basset hound who was the best dog I could have ever had, and I met a beautiful soul in Hawaii.

It was a year after I left my teaching position. I booked a solo trip, and before it, a friend told me that I would meet a man surrounded by gold. Long story short, I met him on the second day of my vacation. His name is Aurelio which means golden. He helped me to heal my soul, and for that, I will love him forever.

Today, life is good. Self-care is my number one priority. I feel fortunate that I have been published in many collaborative works, and I am finishing my first solo book coming out next year. Something that wouldn't have happened if I had decided to end my life. My circle of friends is loving and supportive. I'm excited about life and welcome each new day with a sense of wonder and a smile.

Night after night, I sobbed uncontrollably in that bedroom, wishing the pain would go away. I wanted to end it more times than not. But, I kept going and held on.

Life is worth living. Sometimes blind faith is what is needed in our darkest hours. If you are struggling with mental health issues, you are not alone. When you hear that voice that tells you to wait, pause and hold on. Listen and abide. It will get better.

Chapter

Fourteen

Another Sleepless Night
By Becki Koon

Becki Koon

Becki Koon is a Heart-based Energy Intuitive, Reiki Master, HeartMath Coach, Life Coach, Crystal Practitioner, and Author/Speaker. Through her business, Step Stone, Becki empowers people to seek their inner wisdom while holding space for them to heal, discover, and grow into the next highest version of themselves. She likes to refer to herself as the midwife of birthing a person's remembrance of their divine essence or purpose.

In Becki's work, through Reiki and other healing sessions, Becki receives guidance from not only Jack, her husband who passed, but her angelic guides and family of light, other people's guides, loved ones who have passed, and ascended masters. The world of channeling higher beings is a gift she says is a salve that has helped her deal with loss and grief. Being in service to others through heart-centered action is a gift of the expanded love and compassion she experienced through his conscious death process.

Becki dedicates this story to her love, Jack. She vows to continue using the gifts he so lovingly encouraged her to remember and offer to the world.

Contact:

stepstone2you@gmail.com

www.beckikoon.com

www.facebook.com/becki.koon.consulting

amazon.com/author/beckikoon

Another Sleepless Night

By Becki Koon

I haven't slept. I can't seem to settle into a peaceful state of being, my body restless, my mind revved up in high gear despite the focused breathing techniques I am using. I think you know why, my love. My heart is unsettled. Breathing into my heart, as I have taught so many others, actually hurts right now in my confusion and frustration. I am feeling the tears well in my eyes as I acknowledge how much I miss you, how much I wish you were still physically present, not just in spirit but in the flesh. If you were here, I would not be feeling this sleepless confusion, at a loss to know how to proceed. I am navigating the unsteady ground of developing a new relationship, opening up to another human in vulnerability and possibly love. Yet here I am tonight, sleepless and wondering what the hell I am doing, upset that I even have to tread on this shaky ground, saddened by your leaving this earth plane. Consequently, I do not sleep, and in utter surrender to my wakefulness, I write.

The heart is an amazingly beautiful aspect of our humanity. In fact, I would argue that our humanity resides within the realm of our heart. There are those who say the heart is the seat of the soul, the divine spark that is God realized in form. The energetic power of the heart is measurable, the electromagnetic pulse over 5000 times stronger than the brain. And yet, how many of

178

us have built protective walls around our hearts, hiding behind barriers as we peer through the cracks or from a distance? How many of us hide our internal light, the light of our soul essence, to make sure we don't get hurt by another who might inadvertently blow out the flame, extinguishing our divine connection? At least, that is what our thinking mind will tell us. It happens. I see it time after time in my healing practice and in my own self-assessment, the energetic structures we build over time to protect our most vulnerable human aspect, our heart.

I have been a heart-based person my whole life. It seems to be an aspect of my reality that has always been. I also relate to the term empath, someone who has sensitivity to the mental and emotional state of other people, animals, and situations. Energetic boundaries can become blurred and confusing as to what is mine and what is the other creeps in. Hence, the sleepless night of feeling energies of a disappointment that may or may not even belong to me but are felt in my body, in my heart. And so, I question.

I thought I was done, that my overflowing love was given to the man I adored, my soul mate in this life, Jack. We completed each other, two expressions of a blended soul. We enjoyed a life of spiritual depth and breadth that was noticed by all who were in our presence. His passage into the afterlife was not a known part of our equation, a sudden tear in the fabric of our realities. He was left with 20 days to say goodbye to me and this extraordinary world, while I stood alone on this new life path trying to figure out how I was ever going to mend the huge, jagged tear that ripped my heart to pieces.

I have so much love left to share. It radiates out of my pores. There is still a desire to seek out love, companionship, a partner to share life with, but that desire requires a willingness to be open, vulnerable, and exposed, deconstructing the walls built for protection, the walls I constructed to cover up the open wound.

I thought I had done a good job of grieving my loss, allowing my feelings to flow, not hiding my heartbreak, and moving forward towards a new life, perhaps a new relationship. And then it happened, a dark night in my soul. The darkness seemed to engulf me and I was crying out to Jack that I just wanted to join him.

"Please don't make me stay here without you!" I sobbed beseechingly. "I don't want to be here alone. I just want to be with you, my love."

Our sacred love crosses the veil of dimensions and I often hear him communicate with me. We have not lost our connection and he is with me always. It is as if my voice is a beacon for him that he hears loud and clear. Whenever I need him, he is there in spirit, counseling, or more often than not, consoling me. I am full of gratitude for this undying love and the eternal bond we share.

And yet......

This amazing bond has also led to some deep-seated confusion on my part and a holding onto him in a way that was not helping me want to stay earthbound. It was easy for me to want to join him while I was at the darkest point in my life, missing his presence. Fortunately, the moment passed and I found myself crawling out of the despair. Jack constantly reminded me it was not my time, that I still had other things left to do on the earth plane. I also felt the hand of God, Jesus, Mother Mary, and Mary Magdalene supporting me as I sought help from family, friends, and professionals to move me through another layer of grief, my heart feeling appreciation for the insights I was learning.

And then I found it. A lump in my breast.

I had lost some weight under the stress I had been experiencing. Food was not high on my priority list; especially when under stress, it is hard for me to stomach anything resembling food. The hidden blessing was the weight loss helped me find the lump in my left breast, which was large enough I knew it needed to be addressed. I had a moment of panic in the shower that night as intuitively I felt what was coming.

Twenty months after Jack passed, I heard the word cancer again, only this time it was related to me, not Jack; my breast, not his lungs. The word cancer was challenging my reality once again.

We humans have the capacity to feel many emotions, the heart center offering up a multitude of expressions for us to experience as we navigate our humanity. The feeling of shock can send waves of instant heat and sharp needles throughout the body. The news given by my doctor was no exception. It was what I felt when I heard the news about Jack as we sat in the ER that fateful evening. My shock then turned into a numb sensation as I absorbed what this meant in my current reality. I would be facing some tough decisions.

Life often presents us with choice points that impact our reality and shift us onto another life path trajectory. Was I really committed to staying on the planet? Was I ready to move forward with a life without Jack's physical presence? Was I ready to walk with life and not death, change the outcome from 20 months earlier?

I found I was dancing between the worlds, not really grounded in the physical realm. I knew I had a decision to make. I had to let go of my yearning for Jack in the physical at an even deeper level. I stood in front of his picture and spoke to him through tears streaming down my face.

I have to let go, my love, not a letting go of our sacred love connection but a moving on in my current reality. I desire to live!

In that moment, I made a very conscious choice to stay and deal with what the cancer was showing me. Surgery proved beneficial and, while it was stage three cancer, they were able to get clean margins around the tumor and my lymph nodes were clear.

Living a life steeped in alternative healing, I was navigating all available options and tools. One of the activities I do on a regular basis is free-flow writing. I have a thought or question in mind and then I open up a channel through my heart center and allow the words to flow. When I write from the heart space, I know I am connecting to the divine, the God spark within me. I had already been working with my body to understand what the cancer was showing me, not feeling at all upset with my body but trying to understand the energetics behind the manifestation. No surprise that shock and grief played a role, but I wanted to understand at a soul level what my body was sharing with me. So, I went into meditation, picked up my journal and wrote my truth. Keep in mind that the words are **my** truth and not necessarily anyone else's truth. We are all unique expressions of the God Force. I addressed my body and the cancer cells directly.

What are you here to show me?

Choice, you always have choice. You always have a choice - to heal, to stay stuck, to recognize your divine power, to leave the planet, to stand strong in your own journey, to listen to others' wants and desires; choice not to listen, choice to walk in joy, beauty, and sovereignty despite your life circumstance.

It is your awareness of choice we have shown you. You are listening and we, your body cells, applaud you for your wisdom and strength to step into awareness of what works for you. We want you to love yourself first and foremost. Do not overlook your body. You are learning and when self-love becomes a constant state of being, we no longer need to manifest. Allow your feelings to rise and move through your body. Allow the learning to flow out onto the page as you share with others.

We (cancer cells) are part of a bigger whole, a collective consciousness that can move into a different state of being, but it must be done consciously and with intent. Thus, the healing can take place within (inside the body) as well as without (the collective consciousness). The learning is part of the collective desire to transform.

Many people use our type of cells to leave the earth plane as part of a bigger plan. But, we are not to be feared, to be at war with. LOVE US INTO NON-EXISTENCE. Love us into a transformational energy that cleanses the heart and soul and changes lives. Complete love of self is the key. Can you love that completely, that fully, your body that shows you the pocket of "unwellness" in your breast? We only exist as a modifier of energy, a catalyst for the body, mind, and soul to shift, to change, to expand into something new.

It is your choice - life, death, health, illness, healing, lesson, change, LOVE.

Everywhere I turned, I was being guided back to love, back to the heart, back to the divine essence that is the energy of the cosmos, the compassionate love of Christ Consciousness. I honored what my cancer cells imparted to me that day and have been loving them into non-existence every day since.

Sometimes the breaking open of the heart happens through tragedy, hardship, a dark night of the soul that catalyzes a reckoning. Other times, the opening of the heart happens through joy, laughter, the love of another, children laughing, blissful moments in nature. Of course, we all prefer what feels like a higher vibration, but sometimes the biggest heart openings are the most challenging. Our task is to be willing to see it through the lens of divine love, to allow vulnerability. We all have choice in how we view the circumstances we find ourselves in.

Sometimes choice is fraught with the inability to see clearly what our intuitive nature is guiding us to experience. Recently, I was in a situation where my inner voice spoke to me, and I ignored the inner wisdom. I was teaching a class and someone attended the class who did not feel well. My immediate reaction was to excuse myself from teaching the class; there were other teachers available who could take charge. My intuition said I did not need to expose myself to vulnerability while I was in the middle of dealing with radiation for cancer. Then my thinking mind rationalized away my intuition and my sense of responsibility overrode my inner wisdom. Several days later, I came down with COVID. I became very sick and, at one point, I felt as though I was not going to make it.

The inner wisdom of my soul connection had spoken and I ignored my own voice. I am not blaming anyone but the fact remains that I took the path of ignoring my first impulse, the whisper of my soul wisdom. Do I regret my decision? Of course I do, but I also learned a lot about myself in the process. I am now much more likely to follow the first flush of heart wisdom as it presents itself. It is up to me to understand what my own journey to heart means for me.

Heart consciousness is rising on the planet despite how it appears on the surface. As humanity evolves, we are moving into a closer connection to the compassionate energy of the universe, that of the frequency of love.

There are many tools to help you gain access to the heart space. I constantly use focused breath as conduit for heart connection. By placing a hand on your heart and another hand on your stomach, you access focused attention to the breath. When focusing attention on your breath while feeling into the heart space, the body naturally goes into a state of coherence, a level of peace that calms the body's autonomic nervous system response, thus providing clearer intuitive thought.

Heart-focused meditation is another form of developing a stronger connection to the whispers of the heart. The subtle realms are often found while relaxing into a calm state of awareness. You don't have to be a seasoned meditation expert; just find moments of calm to the best of your ability. The key is to not stress whether you are doing it right. Allow yourself to have a few minutes and rest into your heart, regardless of how easily the mind relaxes.

If you rest into your heart, then you may just find that you can channel or free-flow write. Try this: ask your heart, your higher awareness, a question you would like insight on. Write the question, take a deep breath, and then just write, without thought, without any predetermined set of answers. Allow the words to flow onto the page. You may be pleasantly surprised at what you find written there. The more you test the waters, the easier it is to find flow of information. You bypass the thinking-mind and allow the heart-mind to play.

There are so many ways in which we can explore the realm of the heart. I encourage you to find what works for you. The more you tap into your own unique signature, the more the subtle realm of the heart expands.

I do not claim to have the answers. What I do know is I will continue to strive to open to the possibilities of heart-centered action, allowing vulnerability to be a welcome companion in all aspects of my life. Choice is mine and my goal is to live expanded compassion, calling on the support of God, Jesus, The Mary's, and my higher soul connection.

Jack will be forever in my heart, an extension of the divine love we share. But no matter what life brings for me to experience while on this earth plane, I welcome it with open arms, ready to face the dark nights as well as turn my eyes to the beautiful bright days this messy human life offers.

Whispers from the heart: to listen is a choice.

Chapter

Fifteen

The Crossroads
By Kenneth Laws II

Kenneth Laws II

Kenneth I Laws II has been on a spiritual path after a series of life-altering events in 2013 and has spent his time trying to understand the unexplained, his awakening. Through his search for answers, he has come to realize the true meaning of "oneness," as well as divine events designed to elevate the mind above the ego-driven, fear-based life. Kenneth has come to accept that part of his mission and gift is to write; write about love, forgiveness, and kindness. His first book, *365 Goodness Abounds*, in which he is a contributing author, was only the beginning. His contributions can be found in the book *Inspirations: 101 Uplifting Stories for Daily Happiness* and *365 Soulful messages: The right guidance at the right time* and *Manifestations: True Stories Of Bringing The Imagined Into Reality, Grateful Souls: The Art and Practice of Gratitude.*

The Crossroads

By Kenneth Laws II

H ere I stand at yet another crossroads in my life, trembling with fears of the unchartered roads that lay before me; what do I do, who do I listen to?

Funny thing about life and crossroads; I have come to understand that life is nothing more than a series of twists and turns. Life is simply a series of choices! Do I take a left, right, up, down, yes, no, right or wrong?

Choices

So, where do we get the information to make all these choices, and how do we come to a place of knowing what is the right decision at any given moment? As human beings, we rely on friends and family, the news, social media, our spouses, books, churches, leaders, ad infinitum. I have come to believe that the ultimate guidance in making these choices lies within each of us, all the way down at that gut level. Seeking and finding the answers to all the questions and choices can be challenging at best. And then there are the tough choices, especially as a parent, that we must make. One such example is my wife making the gut-wrenching decision to send her youngest child away for many months to a residential behavioral care facility. But how she arrived at the ultimate decision to do so came in the form of a whisper from deep within her soul to her heart. She found a level of understanding of her limitations as a parent, followed by a knowing that the care her youngest child needed was beyond her abilities. In this example, as parents, we seek counsel from those we trust to satisfy the ego of our mind. Don't get me wrong; there is *nothing* wrong with making an educated decision, especially when it involves a child or a loved one.

In an effort to satisfy the limits of the finite mind, we can say that the whisper or voice from within is the voice of God, the Universe, the Great Spirit in the sky, and my personal favorite, the soul. So, a whisper from the soul, through the heart, and into our minds guide us on the path of life. I believe this whisper is mainly used for our personal well-being and leads one another to live a life of unconditional love. I would be remiss if I didn't mention that self-love must come before unconditional love for others. We must love ourselves and all our flaws first before we can love one another unconditionally. I like to use the phrase, a return to living and loving through the eyes of a child. Can you recall when we were little, and we loved those closest to us with unconditional love, no matter what they did or said? This is the purest form of love and gratitude for the people around us. As we age, we begin to use external factors to determine who and how we choose to love. We begin to look externally for the answers to life and which choices we should make. Unconditional love can be possible when we can return to loving as we did as children.

Soul Seeking

So, returning to living and loving through the eyes of a child and relying on our souls to whisper the knowledge and the answers we need can be a daunting task. I will assume that one of the goals of our human existence is to find peace within to love ourselves and others unconditionally. Another goal should be to find freedom and happiness within that allows us to love and serve our fellow humans. I think this is possible when we live from a soul level. Our souls will eventually seek out their likeness (another soul) to share in this life that we desire. To take this one step further, I think our souls seek to find balance in the Universe. Our souls seek out other souls *unlike* them. What I mean here is that the soul seeks another one where the owner's heart and mind are different. Some may disagree with the above but think about it for a moment; if our hearts and souls sought out something similar or the same, it never presents a challenge. Funny how people can be so very similar and yet so very different. What we find is that it is actually in the differences where the balance lies.

Let us assume for a moment that every human being weighed precisely the same, and we put two people on the same side of a seesaw; it is just going to stay there. There will be no movement; it sits stationary and out of balance. When we put both people on the seesaw, except each one is on the ends, opposite one another, it becomes balanced. Although it may move up and down with the force of each pushing off the ground with their legs, it moves in a very balanced fashion. Souls, hearts, and our minds need exercise to grow. They need movement to grow.

Let's look at a more realistic example of no movement related to being human and our growth potential. If you consistently surround yourself with people who think, act, and believe exactly as you do, there is nothing there to challenge our intellect, thoughts, and beliefs. Many people surround themselves with sameness because it is comfortable and because it is the easy way not to be challenged. Comfortable and likeness are where the mundane and the ordinary lie. It is outside of this comfort zone where real growth and evolution happen. If there were never any challenges or movement, how can there possibly be any mental and spiritual growth?

I do believe our souls are constantly moving in an effort to seek out balance. It is reasonable that the change in seasons is nothing more than movement in nature to grow, evolve, and maintain its balance. Nature has a very cyclical movement, as do humans. They all have to move to grow and develop. This constant movement in humans challenges who we think we are and should be. When we allow it, our souls lead us to who we are and who we are to become, all in the name of seeking balance.

Go back to the thought of comfortable. Change and growth lie in the areas of discomfort, which most humans cannot stand. We must be willing to follow our heart and soul to the one that will promote this very growth and evolution it seeks. My soul knows what it needs; I have to make sure that I listen and follow it.

Life in Reverse

The soul's whisper to the heart is seeking peace in a world
of chaos, seeking balance in a world of imbalance, where it
just wants to play and be free. The soul wants to lead us to
a life of joy and love we have yet to experience. The place
where the words love and surrender become prevalent in
our everyday interactions.

I will stick with the assumption that we as humans desire
peace within to love ourselves and others unconditionally
so that we can play and be free. We cloud this voice with
our ego, our mind, our thoughts, and with other people. All
these things block our hearing so that we cannot hear the
whisper inside. Many are busy trying to control the
outcomes of their lives, shaping and molding it so that the
ending fits the one living in their head. Yes, our lives are
malleable to a certain extent. And yes, I believe we can
attract more positive in our lives with the proper motive,
right thought, and correct action. But we must give up the
illusion that we are in total control of our lives. Living this
way will always create fear and anxiety, and ultimately a
disappointment. When we have these expectations of our
lives, we will always be disappointed and let down.
Nothing will ever be enough.

When we use our minds to dictate what our hearts and
souls need instead of allowing our hearts to listen to the
still small voice coming from the soul, this would be living
life in reverse, and I can speak from personal experience.
Living in reverse will always create fear. This is living
from the egoic mind's place, which is always in defense

mode, constantly making more noise than we need. We must be still to hear it, literally. Our minds need to be quiet and not think of the past or future, but only this moment as it exists. It is in these moments that we listen for the answers to the questions we ask ourselves.

My Crossroads

So back to my crossroads, I stand trembling with fear of the unknown, listening for the small, still voice inside of me. My head was still full of noise, the light of my spirit dim but present. Up to this point, I had been living life in reverse; my mind had been trying to convince my heart and soul that I was living a full and happy life. I know today that my head could not have been more wrong. Since I could not quite hear my whisper from all the noise, the quiet voice came to me from God through another person. They said, "You know what to do; just be still and listen." Something deep within the core of my being shifted, and in that very instant life as I knew it was about to change forever. My mind had come to a place of surrendering to my heart and soul, finally letting go of the facade it had created. At that moment of surrender, I fully accepted the road about to be paved for me. I had a deep knowing that all would be ok.

Each of the roads leads to opposite places related to life, love, relationships, and the pursuit of happiness. My still small whisper says to me, "You know which way to go, one road is much easier than the other, but the easy one is filled with an ultimate pain and suffering and the loss of who I am forever." I was able to continue to be still long enough to hear the whisper. It says, "I will not lead you astray, but you must stay on this path with an unwavering conviction and a knowing that all will be as it should be." As for the other road, the whisper continues and says, "Take it, I know it's uphill, and you cannot see the top but trust me, and I will lead you to a life that people only dream of, the one where your soul finds the other soul it has been seeking."

I had found pure love standing before me in human form. The beauty of true love is that it has no boundaries. It is limitless and infinite. I learned a long time ago that if you must ask yourself whether someone loves you, then they don't. Love cannot contain itself. The love that comes from soul living will express itself in the sweetest of subtle ways. If we use only our minds, we will miss the subtleties, but the soul sees and knows. The point is to have one's eyes wide open and the heart even more expansive, thereby allowing our soul to speak to us and to love who it wants, and more importantly, quieting our mind long enough to hear it.

Chapter

Sixteen

Whispers from the Road
By Paula Meyer

Paula Meyer

After becoming a widow at 54, Paula Meyer left her job and began a year of travel to heal her heart. As her travel ended, the Covid-19 pandemic began. The strategies for navigating the grief of her husband's death also helped with the grief from the pandemic and social unrest. Losing her freedom and lifestyle, she was thrown into the unknown just as her business began. Her new book, *Great Loss,*

Greater Love: The Art & Heart of Navigating Grief, chronicles her year of travel and is a #1 International Bestseller on Amazon.

Paula has 30+ years of experience as an event planner and contracting specialist, with 12 years in author/speaker management. She has organized and managed more than 150 workshops around the world. Her company, GP Eventworx, specializes in event production for speaker/teacher workshops, as well as grief retreats for women. She has traveled to 20 countries, some multiple times, and 42 US States. Her goal is to visit 30 countries and all 56 US States and territories by the end of 2025. You can follow her journey at www.greatlossgreaterlove.com.

Whispers from the Road
By Paula Meyer

In my book *Great Loss, Greater Love: The Art & Heart of Navigating Grief*, I wrote about my year of travel, nine months after my husband Gary died. Traveling through eleven countries helped me to heal my heart. Part of that healing process was an exercise in everyday reverence, where I found three things: Gratitude, Laughter, and Divine.

It's September 2021, and I find myself on another road trip driving through twelve states, re-creating the story from my book. Rather than traveling around the world in this age of Covid, I'm embarking on a US road trip, where I can control where I am, who I encounter, and protect my health and well-being.

I decided to do a Route 66 road trip, to celebrate Gary's 66th birthday and honor his life and our connection. My original plan was to do the road trip in August since his birthday is on Aug. 19th. However, I was also attending an event for widows in Houston in September, so I pushed the road trip out and combined the trips.

"A good traveler has no fixed plans, and is not intent on arriving." —Lao Tzu

Other than the Houston event, I had no agenda to follow. The best thing about traveling without an agenda is the ability to stop whenever I want. I watch for the brown highway signs that indicate something of interest is coming up. If that sign resonates with me, I pull over and experience it. I've learned so many fun and amazing things by taking this one simple action. I left my home in Colorado on a sunny Tuesday afternoon. As I began this journey, the odometer on GT (Gary's truck) showed 203,267 miles.

My first stop is Lamar, Colorado, to see the Tri-State Veteran & First Responders Memorial. It was called the 9-11 Tribute on the sign, and after all the coverage of the 20-year anniversary of 9-11, I was intrigued. It actually was honoring all those who sacrificed theirs lives in the Tri-State area over the years serving their communities.

Road Whispers: A great way to start the journey, given that this trip was about honoring and remembering Gary, and thus would become about honoring and remembering many more.

I drove across the panhandle of Oklahoma in the early evening and made it to Amarillo, Texas, to get on Route 66 and stopped there for the night. The next morning, I began the drive east to Oklahoma City. Driving through Groom, Texas, I came upon a gigantic cross and decided to check it out. As I made my way to the cross, I felt I was being engulfed by it. At the base of the cross was a circular pattern of figures that were depictions of the stations of the cross, the story of the crucifixion of Jesus. At the first station, titled *Jesus is condemned to death*, there was Jesus standing in front of a man sitting on a chair. As I read the plaque, it started with: *Pilate said to them: "Why? What evil has he done?"* I was confused as in my mind, I read "Pilate" like the exercise Pilates. I finally realized they meant "Pilate" pronounced like "pilot" as in Pontius Pilate!

Road Whispers: Words are not always what they seem, especially in our modern world!

I continued my walk around the cross, experiencing each of the stations, and was most taken by the one of Mother Mary wiping Jesus' brow as he fell.

Road Whispers: There are always people and angels around us who are ready to step in and support us when we are in need.

Just outside the circle was a depiction of the last supper, with Jesus sitting at the table with seven apostles. Apparently, the other five were late for supper! Behind this were stairs leading up to three crosses, where Jesus hung on the center cross and two men on either side. Below Jesus' cross were rocks inscribed with people's names and the date they were there, an inspirational saying, or someone who had lived and died.

Road Whispers: Remember the meaning of Jesus' life and death, especially on this trip that was honoring Gary's life and death. All life has meaning.

As I came to Oklahoma City, I stopped at the Route 66 Museum and was surprised to find it was on Gary Boulevard! When I chose this museum, I had no idea of the address; I just bookmarked it because it was rated the best of all the Route 66 museums. When it was time to exit the highway, Siri shared that we would be turning left on Gary Boulevard!

Road Whispers: Spirit and our loved ones are always showing us signs of their presence, and many times in ways that truly surprise us!

I learned that Route 66 begins in Chicago and runs through eight states and 2,448 miles, ending at the Santa Monica Pier in California. The museum was well done, and I learned so much about its beginnings from its commissioned date on November 11, 1926, up to the present day. It's also called the Will Rogers Highway and the Mother Road. Route 66 has changed over the years and was replaced by five interstate highways in 1984. Fortunately, you can still drive many of the old routes.

Road Whispers: Just like life changes, old becomes new, and it was a great reminder to savor the past while also welcoming the new with an adventurous and curious spirit.

I then visited the Oklahoma City Memorial. The memorial was created over the building that was destroyed. A large reflection pool is flanked on the north and south sides with the Gates of Time, one inscribed with 9:01, the other with 9:03. The blast happened at 9:02, so the minute before represents the last moments of peace, and the minute after represents the first moments of recovery. On the east side of the reflecting pool is The Field of Empty Chairs, a tribute to the 168 Americans who were killed on April 19, 1995. There was a daycare center on-site, so there were many small chairs for the lost children. I visited the museum on the west side of the pool and learned about the events of that day. Such a somber and heavy experience, yet very beautiful and moving.

Road Whispers: Remember the power of the human spirit and the bravery of those who risked their lives to save lives. Community spirit and connection are where the healing begins and how we arise out of any tragedy.

I arrived in Houston and got settled in, excited for the weekend to come. I would be attending the Widow's Empowerment Event being presented by the Modern Widow's Club. That evening, I ventured out for a walk and found an amazing Waterwall a few blocks away. As I was walking back to the hotel, I found three pennies together on the sidewalk. I always see coins as a sign from Spirit and picked them up. When I got back to my room, I checked the dates on each penny, as I believe that sometimes there are messages in the dates. They were 1969, 2003, and 2019. The first two dates didn't have any apparent meaning; however, the third one did.

Road Whispers: 2019 was when I quit my job and began my year of travel after Gary died. That was the beginning of my healing journey, and finding this was a reminder and celebration of how far I'd come.

At the event, I met many amazing women going through the same journey as me. It confirmed that I was on the right track, that connecting with other women who are ready to bring joy and meaning back into their lives was the next important step. One day, we did this amazing activity. Coming back from break, we found a plain white plate and a colored marker at our seat. We were instructed to write the things that were holding us back on the plate, and mine were: guilt, anger, fear of success, and fear of failure. Then we carried our plate through a human tunnel of love. As we emerged from the tunnel, there was a large area where we slammed our plates into, breaking it and thus breaking through our fears. It was such a powerful and physical exercise of allowing the negative fear-based energy to be released so that space could be made for a new and higher energy to come in. I connected with many amazing women that I would meet up with later along my road trip, who I know will become life-long friends.

Road Whispers: Find those who can walk with you on your journey and support you as you create your new life. The connection with a new tribe carries us through our challenges.

After the event, I hit the road and set my navigation for Route 66 in Tulsa, Oklahoma. On the way to Tulsa, I found some fun stops. The first was in Denison, Texas, the birthplace of President Eisenhower, on October 14, 1890. It was a cute house, two stories with three gables on top and a big wraparound porch on both levels. I could easily imagine a young Eisenhower running around the expansive lawn while his parents enjoyed watching him from their porch. Off to the side of the house was a large statue of the President in a beautiful garden, with so many beautiful flowers and tons of monarch butterflies flitting about.

In the early afternoon, I crossed the state line back into Oklahoma and arrived in Tulsa. I hopped back on Route 66 and stopped for dinner at a fun restaurant recommended in my Route 66 Guidebook. I stayed in a boutique hotel, where each room had a unique style related to historic Route 66. Mine had a bowling alley theme and honored the architect who built Rose Bowl Lanes as a birthday gift for his wife in 1962.

The next day, I found another birthday gift for a wife in Catoosa, Oklahoma! This roadside attraction was a huge blue whale that was built in a small lake. Driving away from the blue whale, I came upon a 1920's car driving ahead of me and felt like I had been flung back in time to the beginnings of Route 66!

Road Whispers: Life is meant to be fun and filled with whimsy and laughter.

My next stop was the Will Rogers Memorial in Claremore, Oklahoma. His name was familiar to me, but I didn't really know much about him. He was a humorist, actor, cowboy, and a world traveler, just like me! He was also one-quarter Cherokee and much revered by the Cherokee Nation. His life ended in 1935 in an airplane crash in Alaska.

Coming into Commerce, Oklahoma, I visited the boyhood home of Mickey Mantle, where he practiced baseball every day with his father and grandfather. He said he was the only kid in town who didn't get in trouble for breaking a window!

Later that afternoon, I crossed over into Kansas, the smallest section of Route 66, just thirteen miles. Here I found the Rainbow Curve Bridge constructed in 1923 over Brush Creek. It is the last remaining Marsh Arch bridge on Route 66.

Road Whispers: Find inspiration in those who've gone before us. Don't discount the small things!

I later arrived in Springfield, Missouri, where I stayed in another vintage Route 66 motel, one where Elvis once stayed! There were many old-time cars on the property, along with vintage gas pumps and an old red phone booth. I journeyed into the city and found a half-scale model of Stonehenge on the campus of Missouri University of Science & Technology.

Later that afternoon, I arrived in St. Louis and visited the Gateway Arch. It is such an amazing feat of creation! As I crossed into Illinois, I found one of the more spiritual roadside attractions, the shrine of Our Lady of the Highways. The plaque says: *Mary, Loving Mother of Jesus, Protect us on the highway.* It was erected in response to the many accidents and deaths that were happening on Route 66. It's a place to stop and say a prayer for a safe journey, which is exactly what I did! I took two postcards and placed them on my dashboard.

Roadside Whispers: Spirit is always with us; we just need to tune in!

In Springfield, Illinois, the birthplace of President Lincoln, I walked through the Lincoln Memorial Gardens. There was a large and whimsical wooden statue of Lincoln lounging next to a tree. There were many benches with quotes from Lincoln, my favorite being: *The better part of one's life consists of his friendships.*

Roadside Whispers: A wonderful confirmation of the new friends I had just made the weekend before in Houston.

I continued on my journey and ended the day in Chicago, the end of Route 66! I had made it! I was mesmerized by the Chicago city skyline that was lit up so brightly, one of the best city skylines I have seen. I remained in Chicago for three days, enjoying the company of my brother, his wife, and their good friend. We had a wonderful time, eating tons of amazing food, enjoying jazz and comedy, an architectural river cruise, and walking around this beautiful city.

Now that I had completed the Route 66 portion of my road trip, the next week would be visiting some states that I hadn't yet visited, including Minnesota, where Gary was born.

My first stop was Gary, Indiana, where I was greeted by a mural that said "I Love Gary," beautifully created with silhouette images of family and nature. Another welcome sign said, "The People of Gary Welcome You," which made me laugh as I am one of the people of my Gary! I walked along the shores of Lake Michigan and could see Chicago across the water. I found a heart rock and a feather as I walked barefoot along the beach.

Roadside Whispers: Signs are everywhere; do you see them?

At Sleepy Bear Dunes in Michigan, I found more heart rocks and walked along another gorgeous Lake Michigan beach. The weather became colder as I approached the impressive Mackinac Bridge. It was raining and very windy as I bravely crossed it. Happily safe on the other side, I stopped to view the majesty of this engineering masterpiece.

Roadside Whispers: Even amidst the storms of life, there is always beauty to behold.

The next state was Wisconsin, where I made a couple stops in Marinette and Green Bay. My son is a Packers fan, so I visited Lambeau Field and bought some gifts for my cheesehead. Later that day, I met a friend at Paisley Park in Minneapolis to experience Prince's legacy and genius. It was great to see and hear his music on the large stage and get a peek into his life, especially all those amazing clothes and shoes!

One day, my friend and I took kayaks out on Lake Minnetonka, and I spread some of Gary's ashes to celebrate his birthplace.

Roadside Whispers: Amazing people, well-known or not, die all the time. Death is a part of life.

With my road trip nearly complete, I took off on a sunny fall morning. I would travel through three more states to reach home. As I'm driving these final miles, I think about traveling on the road, traveling through time, and being present as we travel through time. I contemplate how this journey has allowed me to enjoy past memories with minimal pain while anticipating future stops with joy and excitement rather than anxiety. I honor myself for the willingness to just pull over when something interesting presents itself, like that geographical marker in Wisconsin that informed me I was halfway between the north pole and the equator.

Roadside Whispers: When we allow ourselves to stop and enjoy what is right in front of us, we learn new things and gain new perspectives. When we can immerse ourselves in childlike curiosity and innocence, we experience joy in the moment. When we can experience joy in the moment, we rekindle our memories of what joy feels like. As we refamiliarize ourselves with that feeling, it starts to come back to us. The more we do it, the easier it becomes, and then we realize it's always been there. Patiently waiting for us to remember it, to invite it back into our lives. We only have to be present. Being on the road is my way of getting and being present.

As I arrive home, GT's odometer now reads 207,891. I'm so grateful for the many blessings and signs I received as I journeyed these 4,624 miles! Ready for the next one!

"People don't take trips — trips take people." —John Steinbeck

Chapter

Seventeen

The Many Ways the
Universe Whispers
By YuSon Shin

YuSon Shin

YuSon Shin is a gifted healer, intuitive, medium, speaker, author and teacher of the healing and intuitive arts based in Los Angeles, California. With her trademark joyful and compassionate demeanor, she uses her gifts to help people and pets all over the world heal, and learn to heal themselves, from a wide array of physical, emotional and spiritual ailments. YuSon is passionate about teaching and holds hands-on workshops where she feels honored to help students awaken their own spiritual gifts and superpowers. She believes everyone has the power to heal themselves.

YuSon is a practitioner and expert in a wide variety of healing techniques because she feels there is no "one size fits all" when working with her clients. She utilizes Akashic records and Chinese energy healing techniques to perform past life, karma and ancestral clearings. She is also a practitioner of the Bengston Energy Healing Method and has hosted Dr. William Bengston's Los Angeles workshop for the past few years. She is a certified Reiki Master (Usui, Archangel & Kundalini) and also uses Integrated Energy Therapy, 5th Dimensional Quantum Healing, Quantum Touch, DNA Theta, and Access Bars. She is an author of *Holistic: 22 Expert Holistic Practitioners Help You Heal Mind Body and Spirit in New Ways* and *Manifestations: True Stories of Bringing the Imagined into Reality.*

You can reach YuSon at YuSon@ShinHealingArts.com and get more information at www.ShinHealingArts.com.

The Many Ways the Universe Whispers

By YuSon Shin

The Universe has a way of tapping lightworkers for service at the appropriate time in our respective lives. It's the equivalent of a divine draft. Some are born with this calling to be a soul warrior, and others are awakened to answer this call to be of service at a later point in their life. We are all born with light, but lightworkers are prompted to turn our "in service" notification on like on a taxi or bus, and we help move people along in their respective journeys. Lightworkers are both teachers and healers but not necessarily in those specific occupations. Regardless of when the call is answered, we have enlisted for duty to help and heal humanity. We are committed to living life lit up from our soul and bravely showing others the way.

However, one of the biggest problems we face as we move from life to life is that as we enter a new life, our memories are wiped clean of our past journeys. We come back in each incarnation, not fully cognizant of our power. As we are awakened, we experience stirrings in our souls and whispers from the heart that we have to decipher before we can actualize our full potential as lightworkers.

Before you convince yourself you can't possibly be a lightworker like I did, please hear this. You are a

lightworker if you have affected anyone in a positive way
and want to have a positive impact on this world.

As you go through the awakening process, it truly feels as
if your intuition comes more alive and can no longer be
ignored. As we are awakened, we feel pushed or pulled
onto the correct path, albeit with lots of pit stops and
detours because life is about having experiences and
making mistakes, and each of these experiences engages
and exercises our intuition. Our hearts sing when we are on
our path. And when we are off course, we feel our hearts
cry so that course corrections can be made. Similar feelings
arise in our gut as we feel strong and sure when we are
headed in the right direction, and conversely, anxious or
weak when we head away from our path. These whispers
and feelings are often referred to as our "calling," and we
feel compelled to answer with action. As we live true to our
heart's calling, our inner voices grow louder but are
sometimes drowned out by the day-to-day noise of our
lives. Meditation is so beneficial because it helps to quiet
the noise in our minds and from the outside world so we
can hear the directives emanating from within.

As soul warriors, we rely on our feelings to determine if we
are on track. At points in our lives, fear may overpower and
confuse us. When this happens, the Universe steps in and
manifests synchronistic signs to appear in greater frequency
so that we can find our way again. However, during our
time of awakening, when we haven't had enough
experiences to feel surefooted in life and our calling, it
feels as if no amount of validating signs from the Universe
can ever be enough to combat the rising feelings of
uncertainty and discomfort. It's natural to want more signs

because it feels magical and special. While feeling special may sound like it's coming from a place of ego, lightworkers are concurrently put through "the ringer" and must endure a wide variety of challenges in life, which include traumas, as training for future work. The challenges have to happen so we can overcome them, heal ourselves and grow wings (sounds better than "balls"), and can relate and be relatable to help others. During these struggles, it feels particularly meaningful to have our most painful moments validated with signs which confirm for us that there is a purpose to the pain and that our lives have meaning.

The Universe has a way of giving us signs that validate our intuitive feelings and confirm that we are on the right path. Here are some subtle ways of communicating:

1. <u>Synchronicities</u> – When things fall into place, such as if you need something and someone offers it to you, or you think of a friend, and they call.
2. <u>Everything flows</u> – When your purpose and desires are in alignment and what you want manifests quickly and easily.
3. <u>Repeating actions</u> – The same circumstances, issues, people, and dilemmas keep arising in your life until you understand the lesson that needs to be learned or the message that needs to be received.
4. <u>Repeating numbers</u> – Repeating series of numbers keep appearing everywhere you look to alert you to pay attention because they have special meanings and messages.

5. Dreams or Déjà vu – Sometimes, our subconscious mind is in a better position to receive messages while we sleep than our conscious mind while we are awake. We are then alerted to these subconscious messages when we experience senses of "déjà vu."

6. Recurring phrases or words – When the Universe wants us to understand and heighten our intuition, it repeatedly sends meaningful phrases or quotes in sometimes the most unexpected places like license plates, trucks, billboards, menus, and more!

7. Pain & Illness – Sometimes, we experience pain and illness so that we can heal from it and recognize the same pain and illness in someone else to better relate to them and help them heal and vice versa.

8. Sounds – When the Universe wants to send us a message, it often sends it in the form of sounds or songs, such as the sounds of bells or songs with meaningful lyrics containing a message or reminding us of an experience.

9. Gut Feelings / Gut check – Often, our bodies know more than our conscious mind. The way our body feels in a situation can often tell more about a universal truth than the logical thoughts in our brain.

10. Delays/Blocks/Resistance – These can come in a variety of forms, both internally, such as procrastination or health issues, and externally, such as a closed street blocking your way or a locked door, are the Universe's way of telling you "This isn't what you should be doing." Some things are just beyond your control, no matter how much you try to bend the world to your will.

I have spent many decades traversing this path as a healer. However, I often forget what it took to get myself to this point and how often I doubted my feelings, questioned myself, and then asked the Universe for validation to continue forward on this path. I often think that my story sounds and feels very different from the story of other healers as they came into their own. Sometimes, in moments of personal doubt, I feel that, somehow, I failed to recognize most of the signs that the Universe sent to me. However, when I review the list above and reflect, I'm reminded that I've received every type of sign, and I'm comforted in the knowledge that I'm exactly where I am supposed to be.

It's common for lightworkers to experience significant spiritual events during childhood. Theresa Caputo, the Long Island Medium, says on her website, "I've been seeing, feeling, and sensing Spirit since I was four years old." That just isn't my story. I don't remember feeling anything of an intuitive or spiritual nature when I was a child. I would not have even put myself in the category of a sensitive person in the first half of my life.

However, there were three "weird" and "out of the ordinary" occurrences that I recall from my childhood. First, I recall having conversations with God in my head for as far back as I can remember as a child. Instead of praying, I would just have talks with God in my mind, and I always heard or felt God was talking right back to me. This was before my family ever went to our Presbyterian church and told me how to pray. I did it without instruction. Second, up until about 13 or 14 years old, I had dreams about how events in my life would unfold, then what I dreamed would

come true in real life, and as I was living it, I felt a dizzying
déjà vu feeling. Third, I sometimes heard my name called
when no one was around. My name is YuSon which
rhymes with Tucson but not very many names or words
resemble the sound of my name. However, I clearly and
distinctly heard my name called by both male and female
voices. Sometimes it sounded like a far-away voice, and
other times it felt as if the person saying my name was right
behind or beside me.

After I experienced sexual trauma at the age of 16, I was
angry at God for not protecting me, and I refused to talk to
him, and I shut down. I was so angry that I went to the
other extreme and declared that myself an atheist because I
felt that God had abandoned me, so I decided I would do
the same to him and myself. It wasn't until I was about 19
years old when I started to hear God and my heart
whispering to me again. They sent me not-so-subtle signs
too. As I walked around the UCLA campus where I was a
student, within a short span of a few months, I was
approached by six or seven religious "bible thumpers"
asking me if I knew God. The first three or five times, I
was dismissive, but around the fifth or sixth time, I started
to feel that God was reaching out and, more importantly,
that I was ready to talk again. I asked friends if they saw
the bible thumpers on campus, and not a single one was
approached except me. Shortly afterward, I started
repeatedly seeing 1111 or 11:11 on the clock twice a day
and 444 everywhere. And right now, as I write this, the
Universe is sending me repeating 1s, 4s, 12:21, and 1234
daily.

Pain doesn't whisper, but it does get its message across by screaming. After many years of unexplained pain in both my feet (the pain would alternate between both feet), I finally concluded that Universe wanted me to heal my feet, heal myself, embrace my intuition, and teach intuition and healing to others. My feet hurt because, spiritually, I dug my heels into my old position of resisting the call to light work. I wanted no part of that, and by God, I went into it kicking and screaming, but finally, I did it, continue to do it, and of course, I haven't had problems with my feet ever since. I am immensely grateful for all that my pain has taught me.

Throughout my life, my heart would lead me to certain strangers, and they often felt safe enough to tell me their intimate stories and secrets. The act of unloading started the healing process. Just acknowledging and validating someone else's struggle while confirming they are not alone can be life-changing. I've always loved that animals and children were drawn to me, and the feelings I would get from being in their company would make my heart sing. These heart songs are loud and proud.

When I was a "newbie" healer, I asked for signs from the Universe to validate my feelings of where my life was headed. I had been taking classes on various healing methods since my 20's, but I felt it was just for my interest. However, in my 40's I felt compelled to dive deeper. Even though I knew I was meant to be a healer, the idea of being psychic or using my intuition seemed foreign and beyond my abilities. The Universe kept sending me quotes from people I respected within a very short timeframe. Albert Einstein's "The only real valuable thing is intuition." Steve

Jobs of Apple Inc. said, "Intuition is more powerful than intellect." Richard Branson's, "I rely more on gut instinct than researching huge amounts of statistics." I saw these quotes over and over again. Being a practical person, I made the connection that tapping into my intuition would be my next step. Once I got it, I didn't see the quotes anymore. I was guided to heighten my intuitive superpowers because they are the foundation for my healing abilities and my life.

Years later, I kept getting a nagging feeling (another way the heart whispers) that I should be healing full-time in addition to my full-time corporate job as a paralegal. This would mean my life would become extremely busy, and I wasn't sure I wanted that, so I asked for a validating sign, specifically a hummingbird feather. I felt it was a good sign to request because I had never seen one before, and hummingbird feathers are not commonly seen. However, a few weeks later, I saw a tiny feather at the bottom of the stairwell that leads to my apartment, just as my dog Peanut and I were on our way out for our morning walk. First, I couldn't believe that my terribly near-sighted eyes had spotted this teeny, tiny feather. Then, I couldn't comprehend that it was indeed a hummingbird feather. So I reissued an amended request to the Universe to show the feather coming right off the hummingbird's butt! A few weeks later, during my morning walk with Peanut, I felt a hummingbird fly within a foot of my head, and when I looked back to see where it came from, I found two hummingbird feathers floating gently down to the ground. Thanks, Universe! Message received.

Up until that point, I had only waded ankle-deep into the healing profession, and that magical sign of a hummingbird feather led me to dive headfirst. But even more magical than signs from the Universe is how when one is aligned with their life purpose, everything seems to flow effortlessly and manifest quickly with very little resistance. In my case, my client list grew, and my schedule was booked without much effort or marketing. As of today, I've had the honor of helping hundreds of people get unstuck and find their way back to their life's purpose and path. The crazy thing is that when I feel burnt out, or I have something big come up in my life, the client schedule always lightens up to fit my need and give me the requisite space to rest, then my schedule fills up again when I'm ready. God and the Universe always have my back no matter what I need, when I listen to the whispers from my heart.

Chapter

Eighteen

The Power of Yes
By Lindy Chaffin Start

Lindy Chaffin Start

Entrepreneur coach and marketing maven Lindy Chaffin Start provides entrepreneurs with insight, strategy, and advice to help them identify their highest purpose and passion and achieve their business goals. She creates marketing strategy and creative as unique and authentic as their company that builds trust with their audience.

You can reach Lindy through her website at www.unstoppablestart.com or via email at lindychaffin@att.net.

The Power of Yes
By Lindy Chaffin Start

D o you remember when you were a small child, sitting at the dining room table with your parents, facing down the Brussels sprouts your mother had put in front of you? There you sat, arms folded, stubborn, begging and pleading not to have to eat them.

"Why don't you want to eat them?" your mother would ask.

"Because they're gross," you'd reply.

"But you haven't even tried them yet," she would rebut in frustration.

I imagine the argument ended one of two ways: 1) you got your way and never had to try the Brussels sprouts, or 2) like many of us, your mom and dad made you sit at the table until they disappeared, meaning the dog ate them.

Let's look further at scenario number one. Okay, six-year-old you is off the hook, but what happened when 26-year-old you tried Brussels sprouts for the first time—flash-fried, crispy, toasty goodness with horseradish aioli to dip them in? Were they delicious? Yes. Yes, they were. And did you regret not trying them sooner? Maybe you did. I sure did.

Now, think about how many times in your life you have said no when a yes could've led to more fun, more joy, more peace, more abundance, more wealth, more love.

Why Do We Say No?

Now that you have a mental list of all the times you've said no, and you really wish you'd said yes, think about why you said no. What made you do that?

Brussels sprouts aside, I can think of so many times I said no. No to the adventure. No to something new. No to being open for someone. One time I even said no to going kayaking down the Ocmulgee River with a group of friends because my husband had promised he'd teach me first, and he never did, so I was afraid of embarrassing myself in front of my friends.

I look back on that moment every time I am faced with making a decision.

Fear stopped me from saying yes. Sure, embarrassment is awful, but it wasn't embarrassment that stopped me. It was the fear of being embarrassed.

Fear can be debilitating for anyone.

People who have suffered trauma fear that it may happen again, which could lead to them never wanting to spend time with people or even leave the house. People who have experienced injury fear that it could happen again if they try that same activity, whatever it may be. The adage "if you fall off a horse, you must get right back on" holds true.

I wanted to sing from the time I was a very small child. I dreamed of being Olivia Newton-John: wearing her gorgeous clothes, getting up on that stage, and singing for the world to hear. Alas, the fourth-grade talent show, where I stood on stage in front of my friends and their parents belting out Irene Cara's "Fame," left me afraid to sing karaoke, much less emulate Olivia Newton-John. I'll never forget the feeling of their stares as I sang along.

The fear of feeling the achy nervousness, the judgment and criticism, and feeling not good enough has kept me off the stage, and from living a full life, up to this point, but no more.

When We are Stuck

The other day, I received an extremely sweet note in the mail from my best friend. You see, I've been going through what feels like a very "stuck" period in my life. I wholly believe in the power of intention and gratitude, and I try to spend a lot of time connected to my higher powers. For me, that brings joy, peace, and freedom. But for the last year or so, I've been very disconnected, to the point of agony. The painful disconnect has led to my business waning and my creativity lacking. Don't get me wrong, my life is far from miserable. I have a wonderful partner and a daughter who make me proud every day, but the "spark" that makes me who I am seems to have gone away. It wasn't until I received my friend David's note that I realized what had happened. Here is what it says:

A wise woman once told me to visualize the life you want...I know you're going through a bit of a rough/lost patch right now but take a second to look around you — you did all that and more. Never forget that. You'll get those innovative juices flowing again. I believe it!

David, in his infinite wisdom, reminded me that I managed to raise a child on my own, I started a business from nothing, and it has grown to a successful boutique agency, I purchased my second home on my own and now get to share it with my daughter and partner. I couldn't be more blessed or grateful.

But with David's words, he reminded me how I got here. I started saying yes. I began to take risks, outcomes be damned, because I knew if I didn't take a chance on something, I would never achieve a thing.

You can start saying yes too. Here's how.

Face Your Fears

To face a fear, you must first recognize it. Go back to the beginning of this story. Take some time, a journal and a pen, and write down all your Brussels sprouts. Seriously, make a list of all the times you said no to doing something that you wished later you would've done. Trying that food.

Buying that dress. Getting that massage. Answering that call. Offering that product. Painting that picture. Whatever those "noes" were, think of as many as you can and make that list.

Now, take a break. The thing about fear is that it will not want to be challenged. It's going to get into your head and tell you all the things it thinks will keep you from doing the next step. It'll tell you that you aren't good enough, that you don't deserve the things you desire and do you know what? Fear is wrong. You are a magnificent being with hopes, dreams, intelligence, and the potential for so much joy. You are good enough. You do deserve what you desire.

Repeat after me: I am good enough. I deserve what I desire.

Got it? Fear can't hold a candle to you.

Now you have your list of noes. Start at the top and take as much time as you need. Hours. Days. Take that very first moment you said no and figure out why. No matter the feeling or emotion that went along with the no, the underlying reason you refused was fear.

Embarrassment = Fear

Pain = Fear

Judgment = Fear

Lack = Fear

Rejection = Fear

Confrontation = Fear

Let's look at another example. When I was fifteen, I went to an amusement park with my friends. They all loved riding roller coasters and asked me to ride with them. My mind raced with fearful ideas: we'll get stuck, I'll fall out, I'll get hurt, someone will die. Good heavens! Fear can be a mighty powerful influence when she gets in your head like that. Someone's going to die if I get on this roller coaster. Really? So, I watched my friends ride and laugh and have the time of their lives. No one got stuck, fell out, got hurt, or even died. Instead, their hearts raced with excitement and joy. And mine could have, too, if I had not let fear stop me from experiencing the moment.

Go through your complete list of noes and write down what could've been different had you said "Yes!"

What would've happened if you had taken that job? Where would you be now? How different would your life be? Just think about it.

What if you had made a business out of selling your art? Would you now be teaching classes? Selling your art in many various formats? Would you be famous?

Did you say no to going on that girls' weekend and miss out on meeting the man of your dreams? How could your life have been different if you had just said yes?

This is not an exercise in uncovering regret. This is how you realize that your thinking needs to shift.

Surround Yourself with People Who Believe in You

Have you ever noticed when you are sharing your excitement about something with someone how their reaction either propels you to keep moving forward or to just quit?

Did I strike a nerve?

You see a lot these days about surrounding yourself with non-toxic people. Self-care has become a huge part of surviving our current times. We often forget that the people we choose to spend time with are part of that self-care routine. But are the people who may pooh-pooh your brilliant idea truly toxic? There's a subtly to friendships that leave us questioning ourselves and our beliefs. I don't believe these friends were put in our circle to be all laughs, drinks, and parties. I believe we need friends who might question our path, direction, and ideas. They aren't there to instill fear. They are merely asking questions about our intent. The fear lies within you.

Ready for another example? In recent years, I was broken-hearted by a friend who couldn't fathom my belief structure. She is an outright atheist. Cool. You do you, babe. Me, I believe in both science and spirit. I'm a God, Universe, guides, angels, and ancestors girl all the way. One day we got on some random topic with another friend about how what we think influences our surroundings. Call it the power of intent or the law of attraction. When I shared my thoughts about how these things work together in conjunction with quantum theory, she literally laughed in my face. Laughed out loud in a coffee shop full of people. I'm sure I turned red in the face, partly from anger and partly from humiliation, but I responded with what I hoped was grace. I was hurt. I was afraid. Could she be right? Could what I believe be wrong?

Are you wondering if we are still friends? Yes, we are. I love her to this day for laughing in my face. She is that friend who challenges me, but I allow her challenges to make me stronger versus giving her the power to take away everything I believe in, especially myself.

It is important to surround yourself with people who lift you up and people who challenge you. The difference lies in how you perceive them and how much control you allow them to have. Let them pooh-pooh. Let them question. Let them say, "Hell yes! Do that!" Just take all of it into consideration and say yes to doing what is right for you.

How to Start Saying Yes

Are you ready to start moving forward by saying "Yes"? Excellent! Here are the most important things to consider.

Evaluate Risks

I'm not going to lie and tell you to invest $10,000 that you don't have into something that is not certain. Heck, I'm so cheap; I started my business with $500 I had in savings. But I want you to do this: the next time someone invites you to a concert, or an amusement park, or to sing karaoke—weigh the risks. Is it going to actually cause you or someone else harm? Not likely? Go for it! Let your hair down and let your heart race. Can you actually die from embarrassment? No? Excellent; get up on that stage! If someone asks you to jump out of an airplane or try base jumping, well, those risks may carry more weight for you if you are a single parent or provide care to a sick child or aging parents. The point is, don't say no because you are scared. You may be missing the most important moment of your life.

Make a List

It's time to take a good long hard look at your life. What opportunities have you missed? Is there anything on your list of noes that you would like to go back and do now? Is there an opportunity staring you in the face that you just can't pull the trigger on? Now is the time to make it happen.

I've always found that by revisiting the little things from the past, facing the little things you were afraid of first, you are more available to move forward. So, if you didn't buy that outfit because you were afraid to spend the money, do yourself a favor and go buy a nice outfit that will make you feel beautiful. If you didn't go to that Ethiopian restaurant because you were fearful you might not like the food, call your bestie and go give it a try. If you refused to go kayaking for fear of embarrassing yourself, go take a class at an outfitter, then call up a friend and go exploring.

Start with the little things. Build your confidence. Discover that you can have fun without dying. Live a little.

Take On the Next BIG Thing

Imagine someone comes to you and says, "I want you to be part of this great opportunity. There is very little investment (under $200) other than time. You would be magnificent. We could work together. You could work part-time from home." Would you jump right in with both feet? Of course not. You would evaluate your risks, which in this case are minimal, and you would decide if you had the bandwidth to make it happen. Would it bring joy to your life? Would it give you the means to accomplish your life's goals? Could it make life fun? Does it fit within your core values? Do you have, or could you obtain, the skills to do it? Can you visualize yourself being successful at it?

If the answer to any or all of these questions is yes, then it's time to create an action plan. Break the new opportunity down into manageable chunks that can be completed within certain amounts of time: 6 months, three months, one month, one week, one day.

Say you want to start selling your art. What are things you would need to do?

- Choose a name
- File for a business license or incorporation
- Reach out to friends and family to discern interest
- Build a website
- Determine products and pricing
- Determine marketing funnels

- Do some grassroots marketing

- Create your social media

- Open for business

It looks like a lot, but you can assign an expected date of completion to each of these action items. Let's take another look at the list with a timeline:

- Choose a name – December 2021

- File for a business license or incorporation – January 2022

- Reach out to friends and family to discern interest – January/February 2022

- Build a website – March 2022

- Determine products and pricing – April-June 2022

- Determine marketing funnels – July 2022

- Do some grassroots marketing – July-August 2022

- Create your social media – August 2022

- Open for business – August 2022

Depending on your bandwidth, passion, and level of stick-to-itiveness, this timeline may look tight, or you may be thinking, "I can get this done before the end of the year." Either way, you can see on paper how breaking things down into manageable chunks can help you move forward.

It's Time to Say Yes

Remember our mantra? "I am good enough. I deserve what I desire." There is no truer statement. I have faith in you. I believe a life awaits you that is full of joy and excitement. It is never too late to start the journey of "Yes." It's time to let go of fear and live.

I hope you will take time each day to remember all the horrible things fear did and said to you and laugh in its face.

Now, say YES!

Acknowledgments

Thank you, God, angels, guides, and ancestors, for Annelise and Andrew and the inspiration they provide me daily. Thank you, David, for always supporting my "yeses." And thank you, Melanie, for being my editor and rock.

Chapter

Nineteen

Learning to Listen
By Janice Story

Janice Story

Janice Story is a gifted Certified Reiki Master Teacher who has experienced a tremendous amount of trauma from an early age. As Janice moved through her own healing, she was able to release 45 years of that trauma, and she uncovered the importance of discovering the value of her own pain and suffering. A decision unfolded to utilize her experiences, channeling them into a source of healing for others.

A lack of support, guidance or a safe haven fueled a desire to be that for other human souls. Through meditation, Reiki Practice, and horses, along with the tools and knowledge she has gained, Janice learned how to feel, express, release and embrace her own journey. Now it is a gift that she feels honored to provide to her clients and students. Janice's compassionate and gentle spirit provides safety for others, and she is able to walk with them to help them overcome their own fears and trauma.

Janice also has a strong connection with her horses, and they have always been a big part of her own healing. She loves to bring them in to work with clients. With the presence and unspoken language of her horses, together, they are able to help create an opening for healing and transformation to occur in ways beyond that of human contact alone.

Janice has a beautiful sacred sanctuary in her home for private or group sessions and classes. She hosts workshops and trainings and loves for people to connect with the essence and healing power of her horses. She is also the Co-Founder/Creator of The Freedom Way® Equine Assisted Coaching Certification Course. You can connect with Janice at:

janice.story@me.com

www.janicestory.com

www.freedomwayequinecoaching.com

Learning to Listen

By Janice Story

I've always struggled in the past with fitting in, or even knowing who I was or what I wanted to do in my life. Sure, I had those magical dreams as a little girl of wanting to be a ballerina, and owning my own beautiful dappled gray horse. Then, of course, there was the handsome prince, having a family and a beautiful castle-like house with a white picket fence and stream in the backyard. Somewhere in the midst of your imagination, reality sets in, and life happens. You wake up one day, and all of your dreams suddenly seem too far out of reach, or they get lost in the course of everyday life. Those dreams become forgotten as you step into strengthening what I used to refer to as *survival skills* to assist you in the task of learning to navigate through life. Looking back now, I often wonder how I ever managed to survive, and I realize that I had to rely on my intuition and listen to those little voices inside. Those soft little whispers were always trying to get my attention. Constantly trying to learn to listen to the guidance that was always there, if I was only willing and open to hearing it. It seemed that so many times during my life, I only wanted to ignore the whispers; I wanted them to go away and be silent. Thank goodness, somewhere along the way, I learned to trust them.

As I was growing up, I would often get these *messages,* although I didn't know where they were coming from. They would be so strong that they seemed pretty scary to me. It was almost as if someone was talking to me or showing me something inside my mind. In so many instances, they were almost like *premonitions of some sort*, and what I saw or heard often happened in real life. The most difficult part of having them was that most of them were very unpleasant events that ended up coming true. I clearly remember one in-particular vision that I had, in which my uncle was injured while riding his motorcycle. The scene in my mind was so detailed, and I literally saw my uncle flying through the air during a crash. I cannot remember how long after that vision it was, maybe a few weeks or months, but I strongly remember being told that my uncle had been in an awful accident. When I asked what had happened, I was told that someone had run through an intersection, and he had been hit on his motorcycle and had been thrown over the vehicle. *Hmmmmm*, w*hat the heck*, exactly as I had seen in that vision I had. My uncle was in the hospital for a while, but thankfully he survived and recovered from his injuries, at least the physical part.

I believe I was only eight or nine years old, or possibly younger at the time, and I recall being so scared and wondering if I had somehow caused that accident because of what I had seen. Or was there a way I could have prevented or stopped it from happening? Maybe I should have told someone. All of these crazy thoughts were circling around and running through my head and had me extremely confused. Many other instances like this had occurred, and these unexplainable voices and visions kept getting stronger and appearing more frequently. I quickly became afraid of them and knew there was no way I could ever tell anyone about them. They would never believe me and perhaps think I was crazy. So I spent most of my life learning how to ignore the *voices* and became an expert at pushing them away.

Fast forward many years, I had to learn to start listening to those little whisper voices again to help guide me through life. And wow, it sure was difficult to learn to trust them. Childhood fears would come rushing back in, trying to convince me it wasn't *safe* to hear them. It would take many years to gain an understanding that the whispers could truly work for me and help me if I would only trust and listen. Ahhhh, there is that word *trust*, one of the most difficult words in the English language.

I can recall being in high school when the voices returned, and those whispers started up again. This time they were different, as they seemed to be telling me what to do instead of showing me things. More of trying to guide me or instruct me, it appeared. High school was not one of the greatest and most enjoyable times in my life, that was for sure. On the contrary, it was quite the opposite. It seemed like I was constantly surrounded by chaos and confusion and things I should never have been exposed to. Without going into a lot of detail, I will briefly say that I had started drinking in order to avoid and numb everything that was going on in my life at home. I was not in a very good place mentally at all, and I'm sure I was headed in a disastrous direction. The whispers kept telling me I had to move out of the house and get away from the situation at home. *What?* I was only sixteen. How could I even think of doing that? How would I live? Of course, it would take a bit of time for me to have the courage to trust that was what I really needed to do. Thankfully, I did finally listen, and at sixteen, I moved out on my own. I probably would not be here today if I had not made that decision and had not listened to the whispers I was hearing.

Over the next few years, there would be many times again that I would refuse to listen and sure wish that I would have! How differently things might have turned out for me. But then I have the realizations that during our lives, we are supposed to go through the experiences that enable us to learn and grow. I am now truly grateful for all of the knowledge and wisdom I have gained through all of the challenges I've overcome in my life. Learning to trust the voices can be so difficult, but once you start, they get clearer and speak more often, especially if you listen. If you constantly ignore the *whispers,* they feel like *two by fours* hitting you over the head.

When you are finally in the process and mindset of routinely tuning into and hearing them, they seem capable of tapping into your subconscious mind as well. I was about nineteen years old when I was in a vehicle that rolled over. I was never one to wear a seat belt, as I found them annoying and very restricting. But that morning in particular, for some reason, I had fastened my seat belt on (I'm sure it had to have been that little whisper guiding me). I was driving a gray Ford extended cab pickup truck when I fell asleep, lost control of it and caused it to roll over several times. Thankfully, even if I was not aware of being obedient to some underlying voice, I was fortunate that I did listen, as I am sure that it saved my life.

For the next six years or so, I would find myself getting stuck over and over again in unfavorable situations. Looking back, I realize that those were the times in my life that I either shut the whispers down again or I intentionally allowed them to be silenced. Drowned out by the childhood fears creeping back in, or my own insecurities, or for whatever reasoning, I couldn't hear them.

I would next land myself in a very unsafe and toxic relationship that would eventually *teach* me many life lessons. The biggest one was learning how I did not want to be treated and how I did not want to live my life. Without going into a lot of the details around that time, the voices started coming back, yet I still wasn't listening to them. As things got worse and pretty frightening in that relationship, the voices got louder and louder, telling me to leave. I continued to ignore them, believing I could help this person change, and everything would improve. I pulled out my survival skills for a few years until I was on the receiving end of literally getting a handprint left on the side of my face. *Hello*! As that whisper now felt like the *two by four* screaming at me, *yes*, I guess it was time to open my ears and start listening again. Maybe someday I would learn instead of remaining in a crazy state of this tug-o-war game.

It would take me a long time to be able to fully acknowledge the guidance that I was receiving and know that I would be able to trust again. I set out on an incredible journey of reconnecting with my intuition and rediscovering myself. I started to learn that when I allowed myself to lean into that trust, instead of always pushing against it, that amazing experiences would come into my life. I began to see and would eventually come to know my own self-worth. I had more confidence, my self-esteem would continue to increase, and I started to feel valued.

I met a wonderful man in September of 1991 and married him in April of 1992. What on earth was I thinking? Right? When he asked me to marry him, the thoughts in my head took over. *You don't even know him; it's way too soon; that's crazy.* As I sit here writing this today, I can proudly say that I'm grateful I listened to the soft whispers from my heart twenty-nine and a half years ago and not the voices arguing inside of my mind. We've created an incredible family and an amazing life together. Our house isn't exactly the castle that I imagined, and we live in the desert, so there is no creek in the backyard. But we do have an incredible place, and my yard is filled with horses. What more could I possibly need or want? Except maybe an indoor arena!

As I continue to learn to trust listening to the whispers, I have had truly incredible experiences come into my life. I became a Reiki Master/Teacher, and I was guided to create a healing room on the side of my house. I have been able to step into teaching and seeing clients right on my property without having the overhead of renting a space. I become an author/speaker and now have contributed stories to seven number one best-selling books. By the time this book is released, it will be eight. I became a mind, body, spirit practitioner and began hosting different trainings and events. I was also given an amazing opportunity to speak during and facilitate a workshop at a Celebrate Your Life event in Sedona, Arizona, in 2019. Yes, the voices would kick in trying to knock me down, making me feel insecure, not good enough. Who was I to think I could do this? The whispers would soon start to override them, as I had found my passion in being of service to others, helping people.

I had started bringing my horses into my sessions with clients many years ago, and it was magical. This is what I wanted to do, Equine Therapy. I was tired of my corporate job. How could I make this work? I had been incorporating everything that I mentioned above on my days off or after work. That corporate job had started to become such a toxic environment for me that it was affecting not only my mental health but my physical health too. The voices kept getting louder and stronger, telling me to become who I was meant to be. How? How could I possibly leave the money, benefits, and security that job was providing? Here I was again, back in my tug-o-war game. With the help of a great mentor, Sunny Dawn Johnston, I made a plan and was able to finally listen to the whispers, at least partway. I stepped down at work so I could keep my insurance and work on building up my business at the same time. Sure, I fought all of the insecurities and questioned what I was doing. Wondering if I could make it, afraid of failing, of not being good enough.

Two years later, here I was, allowing the voices to help me navigate an incredible life. I have manifested a job doing Equine Therapy at a men's rehab center, *Soberman's Estate,* where I can literally ride my horses to work! Who gets to be that lucky? I listened to my guidance and was able to walk away from the corporate job where I had spent twenty-four years of my life. I had been guided to create a certification course for Equine Assisted Coaching so I could share my passion with and teach others to do the same. I partnered with a dear friend of mine, Diana Gogan, and together we created The Freedom Way® Equine Assisted Coaching Certification. I have been able to overcome my lack of confidence, self-worth, low self-esteem and fear. I've found my voice, gained back my feeling of being worthy and have learned to lean into trusting my own intuition, along with those soft whispers. As long as I stay out of fear and continue to stay in a place of trust. Everything seems to work for me instead of against me, and I have been able to create a life where I am truly living.

For the last ten years or so, I have worked diligently to help strengthen my connection to the wisdom of my own intuition, and I've let it guide me. I've learned to discern the difference between the *whispers from the heart* and what I perceived as my ego. I think the difference for me is that if it is coming from your mind and almost like in an argumentative state, then it is most likely going to be your ego driving you. If it is an extremely strong feeling originating in your gut or your heart space, it is probably your intuition guiding you.

How are you going to start learning to trust and to listen to your own whispers from the heart? Here are a few suggestions that may help you:

    * Start some kind of meditation practice so you can reconnect with yourself.

    * Grab a journal and write in it every day.

* Practice gratitude by writing down three things you are grateful for daily.

* Set a positive intention daily.

* Come up with a daily word or quote of the day.

* Surround yourself with others who lift you up.

* Make your own self-care a priority.

* Take some time each day to play.

* Practice loving kindness daily.

Those are a few ideas to get you started. I think the most important one is to have compassion for yourself. Don't beat yourself up. *You are worthy!* It's time for you to create the life you love and deserve! You're right! It's not easy! But take the first step, take some kind of action! Try honoring and listening to your own true *whispers from the heart.*

As I sit here reflecting on the journey that I have been on, I am forever grateful that I finally learned to listen to those amazing little voices inside, "the whispers from the heart." For they have truly changed my life and set me on the path of where I am supposed to be, helping others learn to acknowledge and have the confidence to listen to and honor their own whispers.

Chapter

Twenty

Rewire Your Mind For Success
By Jonny Torgersen

Jonny Torgersen

Jonny Torgersen was born and raised in Oslo, Norway. He moved to the United States in 2009 with a vision for a new life and currently lives in San Diego. Jonny is a board-certified hypnotist. As a result of working with him, people experience significant shifts in their lives, both emotionally and mentally, to be better able to live closer to their inner truth. Jonny's clients report back that they overcome fears that are decades old and become ready to take on new opportunities in their lives. Jonny creates life-changing experiences that allow his clients to have breakthroughs that not only heal but create a renewed sense of happiness and a more fulfilling trajectory in life. His work brings the hopes and visions of his clients to fruition and allows for the internal freedom they desire. Get in touch and learn how to create change in your life and experience breakthroughs in your relationships, finance, and health.

www.northcountyhypnosis.com

info@northcountyhypnosis.com

(619) 786-0660

Rewire Your Mind For Success
By Jonny Torgersen

T oday I live a life of increased abundance in every area of my life. I'm amazed that I get to collaborate and work alongside some of the most influential thought leaders in the personal development world. I enjoy great friendships and regularly rely on my friends for good company, help, and support. I have a successful career and get to touch the lives of thousands of people through my work, and on top of it, I get to be a proud dad to an amazing son! I feel connected to our world and a higher power on so many levels. But what you may not know is that my life wasn't always like this.

Less than ten years ago, in 2011, life looked very different at the age of 25. I was a single dad and an immigrant, fresh off the boat. I had no job or a car to get around. My body still recalls the physical struggle of getting around town with a 2-year-old pushing a stroller. Located in the high desert, Santa Fe, New Mexico, was extremely cold in the winter. I still recall the feeling of warming up my son's hands and face with my own hands. All the while thinking to myself that in the 45 minutes it took to walk from his preschool back home, we'd be able to relax in the warmth. I kept repeating to myself, "Just keep walking a little bit longer. Almost there." The whole time I remember glancing in resentment at all the people in cars passing by. "Why couldn't I have a car? Doesn't the Universe see me struggling over here taking care of this young child?"

The end of each day left me feeling two ways; I was physically exhausted yet so grateful for having taken care of and put my young son to bed. I felt grateful seeing his sweet face sleeping without a care in the world or knowing my daily struggles. I met his daily needs with love and care, and that felt good to me. And this daily routine became my anchor and motivation to keep going—one day at a time. One night at a time. However, one particular morning was all about to change that, and my son would come to learn a whole different side of me.

I recall vividly waking up one morning having the flu and feeling terrible. I just didn't want to get out of bed. As a parent to a young child, there is no such thing as taking a sick day or sleeping in. My boy was hungry and ready for his breakfast. I crawl out of bed and into the kitchen, preparing to make his favorite breakfast. Scrambled eggs! Little did I know I was about to scramble my own morning. The mounting pressure of barely making it, being stuck in a legal process to snatch my American Dream, all while feeling like an overcooked vegetable, was about to get the best of me. On top of it, I just wasn't good at asking for help from my friends. My attitude all along had been, "Nah, you got this, Jonny! You're a strong guy; push against the resistance, no help needed!" The awareness of that particular shortcoming was just moments away from bringing me to my knees.

I'm standing in the kitchen with the pan in my hand when all of a sudden, the pan separates from the handle. The pan clanked on the floor, and eggs scattered all over. As I'm standing there, dirt poor, with a literal panhandle in my hand, I immediately feel a sense of rage and despair overcome me. I start to shout in a rageful voice! "Why God—*why!?* If you expect me to raise this young boy, at least help me out here! I'm all on my own, and I can't even make my son *breakfast!?*"

You see, in my despair, I lost all sense of calmness. I had resorted to the only reaction I knew at the time; a *knee-jerk* reaction. I had no concept of taking a deep breath to calm down my nervous system. Next, I slam the handle as hard as possible in the kitchen sink to alleviate the explosive pressure built up in me. The handle makes a deafening noise as it bounces back up from the rusted metal sink and eventually hits the floor. I'm sure my neighbor downstairs could hear all that was going on!

It's at that moment I notice, in the corner of my right eye, my two-year-old, three-foot-tall son standing there with terror in his eyes. He had just witnessed his Papa have a major meltdown and seen a whole different side of who he saw as his superhero. I will never forget the look in his eyes. I *immediately* get down to his eye level, embrace him, hug him, and tell him I'm sorry and everything will be ok. I gave in, and I truly believed that everything would be ok. A sense of calmness struck through my soul like an immediate download just at that moment as I surrendered. Seeing the fear in my son's eyes got my attention, and I somehow snapped out of it. I realized I had escalated a silly situation to something bigger than it needed to be. In just seconds, he learned that I was, in fact, a human being. It was the only response I could feel like I had some sense of control, but obviously, I had just made the situation worse. And all the while I recognized that I am only human and doing the best I could at the time, it also became clear to me that kicking and screaming like a toddler at any little resistance I faced had to stop!

The real problem was that I was living in reaction mode in response to everything around me. I did not accept the circumstances in my life, and my meltdown was a way for me to feel like I had some power over the situation. I was full of envy and sadness for everything I didn't have in my life. I constantly felt like I didn't have enough, that I wasn't enough. And that I wasn't worthy of having enough.

Just a few minutes after my meltdown, my phone rings. My best friend Alexander was on the other end. "Hey Jonny, I'm at the grocery store and thought of you! Do you want me to get you anything?" Without hesitation, I say, "Yes! I need diapers, food, and flu medicine!" As the amazing friend he is, he just responds, "Got it! I'll be at your house in a few minutes!" It was as if he had somehow heard my cry for help, and I had finally become ready to *receive* it. In the past, I would have told him I was fine and didn't need help!

Sometimes in life, we learn lessons the hard way, often at the expense of ourselves and our loved ones. Instead of allowing things to happen for us, many tend to fight back, be in control and close down our hearts. The lesson for me that day was that I am not supposed to do this thing called life entirely on my own. Here I was, a young immigrant with no income, raising a small child, thinking I was supposed to figure it all out on my own. I learned that it's ok to have people to lean on.

It had to take a dramatic morning for me to realize just this. My subconscious mind was holding on to beliefs I was not worthy of receiving help. While logically, I knew it was normal to ask for help, my subconscious mind believed something completely different. This contradiction often happens when we seek to change behavior. Your critical, thinking, conscious mind has one idea of what's possible, yet your subconscious mind believes something else. And guess what, your subconscious mind will *always* win the battle because it's the dominating part of your mind.

As humans experiencing pain, we often come up with responses and behavior to cope. You see, your subconscious mind is operating to help you feel good and safe. And so, when you create coping mechanisms to feel better, you're telling your subconscious mind that this is the behavior that helps you feel good and safe. The subconscious mind does not care if that behavior is good for you or not long-term. It only wants you to feel good at that exact moment. If it senses any relief from emotional discomfort, then that's what it's going to do—help you find ways to alleviate pain, but only temporarily. And this is what you see in people with unhealthy coping mechanisms such as excessive drinking, overeating, smoking, excessive shopping, overly sexual behavior—you name it. Your mind will gravitate towards any type of behavior that numbs you and helps you feel at ease.

Intense emotional situations often open us up to rewire subconscious patterns. Good or bad. That's what happened to me when I saw my son's reaction to my meltdown. The intense emotion I felt overrode any old stinking thinking about not thinking I was worthy of help. I wish I had known at that time that you can change subconscious beliefs on purpose and develop new and healthy habits that will relieve you of pain.

After that incident, it became clear that the pain of keeping up with that old behavior was greater than the fear of trying something new and different. Most of us are motivated to make a shift only to remove ourselves from pain. And so, at that moment, when I was willing to receive help from my friend, he reminded me that we could allow ourselves to move *towards* help and support. I had no concept of what getting out of my head and reaching out for support was.

There are many ways to interject and disrupt negative thinking and behavior. First, you have to become aware of it and recognize that a particular behavior is no longer serving you. Are there currently any behaviors that you are aware of that stand in the way of your growth and healing? Prayers and mantras can be mighty powerful, too. You can rewire your subconscious mind by repeating positive affirmations. What you think about you'll bring about. So instead of focusing on the problem so much, I want to encourage you to try on one of my favorite pieces of wisdom and prayers that I learned from the legendary life coach Iyanla Vanzant. She says: "Beloved, in moments of trials and tribulations, ask the Universe for help using this simple 3-part prayer:

1. HELP!

2. HELP NOW!

3. Thank you.

Any time you start to notice yourself engaging in negative thinking, simply interrupt it! One of the most impactful ways to create a mind-shift change is to disrupt any negativity from snowballing in your mind. While we're always going to have negative thoughts from time to time, what you *do* with those thoughts will create the change for you. So as you start to interrupt the negative thoughts with the word "HELP," actively surrender. Surrender any effort to figure it out, to force a solution. At that moment, you are giving the Universe permission to take over. Then firmly say, "HELP NOW!" to anchor your commitment to surrendering. When you surrender to the help of something greater than yourself, it will show up. Last, remember always to express your gratitude, even before you see the help. Even before you see the solution. Say out loud, "Thank you." Now you embody receiving the support while the spiritual process has started. When you manifest something before you see it, you will align your cells, nervous system, and soul to the path created *for* you. Your subconscious mind starts cooperating with your conscious mind to put new and renewed energy behind your actions. In other words, the tongue in your shoe and the tongue in your mouth are heading in the same direction, and you can expect to see your path change as you walk it. Remember to repeat this process. Repetition is another excellent way to rewire subconscious patterns.

While your path is unique to you, it doesn't mean you have to walk it all alone. You are never alone. When you surrender to life's purpose and calling on your life, the Universe will have your back. However, as long as you rely on dysfunctional behavior, you're not going to be receptive to receiving help. Instead, you uphold blocks and barriers to keep you from seeing what the Universe is willing and able to provide for you. Yes, it can be painful to open up, but isn't the blessings we can receive when we stay open much more valuable than being stuck in dysfunctional behavior and stinking thinking? From my own experiences, I know the Universe wants us to do well, feel well, experience joy and happiness. It's all there and available to us—we just have to become willing. Willing to receive, and in some cases, maybe we just have to become willing to become willing!

I can not recognize my life as it is today. And I'm not counting the house, the kid, the friendships, the car, or the money as my only blessings because all those things and relationships will constantly shift and change. However, *how* I'm feeling is how I genuinely measure my blessings. I have serenity in my life simply from having learned how to ask for and accept help from people and a Higher Power in my life. This help comes in all forms, so don't think it has to look a certain way because you might just miss it. Mine came in the form of my dear friend giving me a call when I didn't expect it and when I needed it the most. Today I know *I* can reach out and lean on my friends and support network *before* I have a meltdown.

I have developed immense trust in life and honestly believe life is *for* us. Your inner mind *wants* you to feel good, safe and protected. And so, your subconscious beliefs will always dictate your behavior and actions based on those ideas. I'm astounded witnessing my clients' lives change when their two minds align on a path of singlemindedness, reaching a new goal. They shift from saying *if* I can get through to *how* I will get through it.

So just as my then 2-year old son witnessed my pain that one crazy morning over 10 years ago, today, I am a witness to *his* challenges whenever he needs me. I can't always fix the problems for him, but I genuinely believe my biggest mission as a dad is to show him how to ask for help and support to be successful at whatever he wants. At the age of 12, he has learned how to advocate for his own needs, both at home and school. He can ask for a minute to breathe when he needs to process something before responding. I have repeatedly taught him to rely on his physical breath to calm his nervous system when he gets worked up. And what I love seeing is that this has become a subconscious pattern for him. It's pretty incredible to see because life will undoubtedly have moments where we don't always know how or what to feel. So give yourself permission to pause, breathe and surrender. On the other side of the struggle, you just don't know what miracle might show up!

Chapter

Twenty-One

Whispers of Transformation
By Chantalle Ullett

Chantalle Ullett

Breathing Life Therapeutics, founded by Chantalle Ullett, was born out of her experience of alternative healing techniques. At a young age, she was a chronic sufferer of neck and shoulder pain. Massage therapy was her first licensing, but only the tip of the iceberg. Chantalle intuitively knew that massage offered more than a physical answer to a physical problem. The human journey of healing also involves the metaphysical. One of her greatest awakenings to this reality came when she participated in a Linking Awareness adventure, an organization whose mission is to help us become aware of what nature and animals never forgot. We are all interconnected, and how interconnectedness is vital to health and healing. Chantalle believes our independent health is connected vitally to our interdependence in what life offers if we are paying attention. As she continued to explore many more natural healing methods and life-changing experiences, the realization soon followed she was naturally gifted to be a practitioner. While healing certainly takes place in her presence, with the wisdom and skill set to offer so many modalities of healing, perceiving herself simply as a conduit for your journey to healing self. She believes everyone possesses intuition, simply needing awakening. Chantalle is an expert in connecting the body and spirit for self-care sessions that are truly effective and long-lasting; Breathing Life Therapeutics desires to meet the need in the lack of alternative techniques offered throughout Lake and McHenry counties. Chantalle has two adult daughters and enjoys life with her husband in Northern Illinois. Chantalle's contact information: cellular: (815)403-9106. Email: cullett72@att.net

Whispers of Transformation
By Chantalle Ullett

"Everyone has their own experience. That's why we are
here, to go through our own experience, to learn, to go
down those paths and eventually you may have gone down
so many paths and learned so much that you don't have to
come back again." —Prince

Sitting in a chair at the cabin overlooking the stillness
of the lake, a lone loon floating in the calm waters
seemingly ever-present in its surroundings. One
could ponder to themselves, why can't our lives be so
simple? Why must a person go through trials and
tribulations to then hold on to it all? What purpose does it
serve in a person's life? Yet, most people do. As though
holding onto baggage will gain them some honor or badge,
when in reality, it can and does wreak havoc on their body,
mind, soul.

The dictionary defines a whisper as a noun, meaning a soft
or confidential voice. Interestingly enough, whose voice is
it coming from? Our own? Someone else? We have all had
experiences where we whisper to our friends in class at
school or restaurants, bars, or libraries. We not only
whisper to people, but some have been known to whisper to
animals, plants, trees, even to imaginary people, or as I
prefer calling them, sentient beings. However, the question
I have posed to myself is this: Who exactly is whispering to
us when no one else is around? Have you ever had an

experience like this? Does it mean we are going crazy, or is it simply our innate being communicating with us?

There have been many times in my life since I was a young child, something or someone would whisper to me to go forth with a choice or path. At times, I chose to ignore it altogether. "What was the point?" I thought to myself. Yet, as the years went by, the choices and decisions made didn't truly matter; they were all part of the journey.

Life continued as it should. My path wasn't clear. However, I was living a life I perceived at the time as a happy one. I finished high school, went to college, received a degree in a career I thought I wanted. Then got a job within said field, which turned out, I didn't enjoy. I switched jobs leaving me still unfulfilled. During this timeframe, I met an incredible man, which fate brought into my path. We married three years later, shortly after, we moved from our home country of Canada to the USA, which is where we live to this day with our two incredibly beautifully talented daughters. As I was unable to work right away due to our immigration status, thus the choice to stay home raising our daughters was made for me. We were granted permanent residency status about 7 years later. I then chose to return to the working world. All during this time, the whisper I would hear when I was younger, thinking gone, was extremely faint.

As I raised my children and worked, there was a longing for something. What exactly? I wasn't sure. Yet, the faint whisper of my innate was always there. I'd like to think my innate spoke via a very good friend of mine in 2008 when they asked me what I was doing with my life. Explaining I worked as a shift manager for Blockbuster, my friend, unimpressed, bluntly stated they thought I would do more with my life. Hurt and shocked by the statement, I knew they were right. My innate often whispered to me about massage therapy. Interestingly, massage therapy was always a part of my life. In high school, I would spend our lunch break massaging my friends' shoulders and necks. Within a few short weeks of my conversation, I registered to return to school and became a Licensed Massage Therapist.

Since having gone back to school in 2009 to learn about massage therapy, it has been a journey of self-discovery and healing. Who would've ever thought one small decision would have a lifelong impact in such an expansive way. As the years in my career went by, the whisper, or should I say my innate being, became stronger, louder, bolder. I would take continuing education classes geared towards my physical ailments to benefit my clients with the same issues, not knowing or understanding the parallels which existed between myself and my clients. I understood we, as beings, were more than just physical beings and our pain or discomfort wasn't just at the physical level. We are physical, mental, and spiritual beings. It made sense to me how our physical bodies could reflect it. So as time went on, the classes I chose to take reflected this principle. Choosing to study and becoming a certified Practitioner in the Bodytalk system in 2013 versus a class called the Best Technique wouldn't be revealed to me until almost 10 years later.

As I continue still to study the Bodytalk system technique, this modality leads me to further understand how to work with the body on an energetic level. It has also guided me to study another impactful class called Linking Awareness.

Linking Awareness helped me to understand my innate being even more. I would travel to different parts of the world because of a whisper. I truly didn't understand the pull or need to be in these magnificent places. I only understood the urgency of the situation. Linking Awareness was the catalyst in my healing journey. I traveled several times to many places with Loesje Jacob, the founder of Linking Awareness. My first journey was to South Africa. We traveled to many areas, including Adam's Calendar, where I returned "home." Seeing as I have never lived there, this fascinated me. We meditated atop a magical place in the town Kaapsehoop. Traveled to Timbavati for an encounter with the White Lion with whom I connected subconsciously. Onto Krueger National Park, where I reconnected with an elephant companion from a previous life. However, the biggest healing for me was back at the ranch where we were staying. During one of our sessions, we partnered up with a colleague, and we were with the horses. Two majestic horses named Louie and Queenie assisted in my session. While both horses stood in front of us, there was an unexplainable shift transpiring inside of my body, as though they knew there was an energetic blockage within me. Falling backward into the arms of my partner, laying me down onto the ground where I felt Louie and Queenie standing at a short distance over the top of me, holding space for transformation. After the session was over, I thanked my partner and the horses. My eyes, as some described, were much clearer and brighter after the session.

In August of 2016, my husband was in a serious motorcycle accident. After a lengthy recovery, I was led to Indonesia to process this major life event. While there, we traveled to Sumatra at the Ways Kambas Elephant Sanctuary, spent a week downtime on a secluded island in the middle of the Red Sea, then to Borneo for 5 days, where we spent time on a klotok which is a riverboat used to navigate the waters. While in Borneo, we docked at different camps to observe the orangutans. As we walked to the feeding stations, I observed the sound the cicadas made, the vibrational sound they emitted changed, especially when the different orangutans came. The cicadas taught me we each have a frequency, much like a radio station we are tuned into. Our frequency changes as we do when we heal, much like a radio station changes over time to suit our taste in music. My next big healing happened while we were docked and had sessions aboard the klotoks. We again partnered up. While it was my turn to receive a session, all of us were lying on mats. As we listened to the music, receiving, my breath relaxed, my pulsed slowed down, my body went into a trance-like state. I became frozen, paralyzed. I was consciously awake yet frozen with fear at the fact I couldn't move. As I lay on the mat, immobilized without any restraint except for my own will, I leaned into my fear, embraced it. After what felt like an eternity of time, I slowly was able to start moving, realizing a major shift in my being happened. I didn't feel as burdened, the weight of carrying so much pain, grief no longer there. I came to understand in part why I chose to study massage therapy. It wasn't because it was something I thought I wanted to do. The experience I had on the klotok revealed to me, it was in part my destiny to help release the physical, mental, spiritual binds which hold people down.

2018 brought me to Hawaii to dive deeper into the knowledge of the five elements. Thanks to the "Apprentice cards, the five elements of personal transformation" created by Monique Fay. Although we worked with the cards for only a day or two, they permitted me to open up to a whole new realm of discovering who I am as a being. One of the cards I worked with, which reminded me an awful lot of a turtle, unlocked my kundalini. It opened up my divine feminine power, unleashing a power within me I didn't know existed. My being transformed. We spent the next day on the north shore beach on Oahu Island. With the air blowing a whispering breeze in my hair, the Pacific Ocean greeted me with a mesmerizing memory of time spent as a mermaid in Atlantis. The following day during our meditation, as I sat with my back to the ground, my legs leaning against a tree, the earth nestled me into the ground, whisking me back to a time of chaos, pain, and war. I couldn't tell you which war or where I was exactly on earth. Excruciating, burning, stabbing pains, ripping my heart apart. Insurmountable grief in my lungs making it hard to breathe, visions of destruction everywhere. Fires burning, clearing the path for new beginnings. As we ended the mediation, we walked back silently, giving us time to contemplate, digesting the experience during the space on top of the mountain. On our last day together as a group, we took a dolphin expedition tour. As we sailed in the Pacific Ocean near Makua Beach, we were greeted by three humpback whales at a safe distance, snorkeled with dolphins from afar, and met up with the turtle who unlocked my kundalini during my meditation earlier in the week.

I traveled the most by myself in 2019, thanks to my whispers. First, in March, I found myself in Phoenix which is where I worked as support staff for an amazing company called Celebrate Your Life for the International Women's Summit. I spent the month of July supporting my mom while she recovered from surgery on her elbow. This was a significant part of my healing journey. My relationship with my mom was dysfunctional at best growing up. Through my travels and the classes I took, I understood the varying relationships we have with people are all part of it. We each play a role in each other's lives to attain an understanding of our higher selves. My mom played an integral part in one of those lessons. Now it was my turn to help in hers. We spent most of the month talking, bonding, as well as simply spending quality time together. Something neither of us did when I was younger. Throughout our conversations, we discovered how parallel our lives were despite the lack of closeness we had with one and another. Before heading home later that summer, forgiveness afforded us the beauty of closing the book on the dysfunctional part of our particular journey, which in turn gave us a fresh start. Our relationship is forever changed. My mother is one of my closest friends now.

I then flew off to the Bahamas to spend five days with Loesje and some other colleagues aboard a catamaran called Indigo Dreams, which took us to Bimini. There, we spent our days snorkeling in the clear waters with various fish, sea creatures, and underwater greenery. There are two particular days which stand out the most. First, we snorkeled in an area I like to call the abyss. This was the moment I felt total oneness with my surroundings and being. No one else seemed to exist at this moment. Just me, the stillness, the depth of my creation expanding into nothingness yet complete wholeness. The other significant moment was the day we snorkeled close to shore, paired up, and had a session in the Atlantic Ocean. To this day, I am still unwrapping what transpired in those waters. I energetically swam with a pod of over a hundred dolphins unwrapping the strands of my DNA, unbinding my knowledge to feel into another's body following the path of dysfunction, unleashing the ties which bind the person to the pain. It is the most glorious, graceful technique I enjoy using the most with my clients. Yet, I haven't quite gotten all the information to unleash its full potential. However, I know it is coming in due time when I am ready to receive it.

This brings me to now, 2020/2021. The past year and a half have been one of enlightenment, shedding beliefs, thoughts, actions which no longer serve a purpose in who I am. It has only been most recently, the last four months or so, where I have gone thru a period of self-awareness, self-discovery, self-commitment, self-perseverance, gratitude, embody-ment, most of all, daring to be me. Quite recently, thanks to a dear friend with whom I shared a few lifetimes, I was able to connect with some of my guides, who have empowered me to dive deeper into my self-awareness. They reminded me of a phrase I frequently tell my clients: "The only person who is going to take care of you is you." My body also reminded me of the importance of self-care in April of this year when I found out I had a compressed disc in my neck. Since that moment, I started listening more intently to my whispers. I don't question or doubt the whispers anymore. Just recently, I returned to the Skamania Lodge in Washington State to work a Celebrate your Life seminar where Dr. Sue Morter was the sole presenter for the weekend. Unbeknownst to me, her father's work is the class I opted not to take almost 10 years prior. She has expanded on his work and taken it further, which to me means, I am meant to learn it now. The five days I spent during that seminar have forever changed me. Part of me was left behind forever. I feel lighter, freer. It is as though I see life clearer. I am continuing my studies with her, as I have more to learn from the Energy Codes she teaches.

I love my husband and daughters deeply. I have given of myself my entire life. I've put my parents, friends, family, and clients before my needs and wants. However, this is my time. My time to give equal importance and efforts to the needs of myself along with those of my loved ones. I am taking advice that I so confidently give to my clients because the only one who can truly take care of me is me. I am continuously growing and expanding my knowledge. The focus has shifted to owing it to myself to be bolder, to shine, to pursue my dreams. I am following my path, discovering my purpose to my higher enlightened self.

My questions to you are these: What are you waiting for? Are you not worthy of your self-happiness?

All of this transpired in my life because I chose to listen to the whisper.

Chapter

Twenty-Two

What's Love Got To Do
With It?
By Patricia Walls

Patricia Walls

Patricia Walls is a natural intuitive living in Texas with her husband and fur baby. Through her natural gift of communication, she works with all life to assist in healing, balance, and expansion. Her training began some 40 years ago in shamanism and evolved through learning and practicing many healing modalities. She has served as an international speaker, teacher, women's retreat leader, healing facilitator, mentor, author, and artist. She just completed her first solo book, *Feeding the Wolf Within,* and is working on the second *Conscious Enlightenment and Expansion,* both offered on Amazon. She continues her earth traditions in making and offering ceremonial sound tools. Her websites include PatriciaWalls.net, GalacticFrequenciesofLight.com, and EarthWombyn.com.

What's Love Got To Do With It?
By Patricia Walls

Have you ever paid attention to how people respond to you? How you respond to them? Notice those triggers, whether it's inside of you or outside of you.

Many of you have seen so much pain in your lives and those around you. If you watch the media, which I don't, you have noticed the patterns. And you are seeing them shift now. Humans are waking up. Wanting to clear up their lives. Wanting to know more, be more, from a spiritual sense.

You are the light. Your light quota has increased if you have done the work. When light shines on the truth, the darkness is the lie that has to come to light, right? The old story that says this can't be, I'm this small thing on this job, in this relationship, I miss whatever, and then the light shines on that and says, "No, you're so much more." And anything you were worried about on the outside has shifted. The control mechanisms, the control triggers are being transmuted. They are no longer needed or effective.

You're going to see it for the next few months. Just from the healing frequencies from all of the stories and inspiration in this book, you will find that it's going to be hard for the people that aren't ready for it to be in your fields while it is going to be very easy for you.

You may ask, "Why the next few months?" You might notice how just yesterday was so much lighter than a month ago. Everything has speeded up as human beings awaken, heal, and expand. And based on the Hundred Monkey Theory, when one wakes, another wakes, and it has the domino effect. So, where it took years of meditation and discipline 20 years ago takes weeks now to accomplish.

There are truths being revealed all around you that you didn't notice before because you weren't awake and aware. You are here; you found this book, this body of collected work because your light quota was increasing, and your higher intelligence was whispering to you, "But wait, there is more."

Yes, you might still see those distortions and darkness. They are always there. They have always been there. The difference is that now you see them, but they don't affect you. And, yes, you can transmute it. It is only energy. It is only frequencies. There can be no darkness where there is light. Only shadows.

Remember those horror movies where you hear the scary music before you see the scary thing. The scary music is the precursor. What if when you get that "feeling of impending doom," you shine light, increase your light quota instead of waiting for the scary thing to appear? If you increase your light quota, the scary thing disappears because you will no longer be on its radar. Your job is to get that you're just here. That you *are* the light. You're just here. Just stay in your power. Stay in your presence to just be the light.

Because you are the light, you may have more darkness come at you. You might have said, "I feel the most darkness I've ever felt in my life. I don't know if I'll ever get over this one." Then, an hour later, the energy has shifted, and you don't know where it went. It's just like the final purge.

You won't relate to things the way you used to. The triggers are less or different as they shift. Food, entertainment, even relationships will shift. People will fall away from you as well. Yes, some of you will be in resistance to that. So many things that don't work are falling off of you. All of the patterns that would have drawn to, created, and sustained those relationships and friendships will shift and fall away.

There are many in my own circle who are no longer here. I miss them. I also know that if they were still in my circle that there would be disagreements, distention, and disharmony. That is what I have moved away from the need to create. I am not necessarily saying that they live in those environments. Sometimes it is our combined energy that creates those environments. Away from one another, we create differently. Have you ever been in a relationship where the person just makes you want to scream from frustration? When they are not with you, both of you are calmer and happier. Sometimes you have to let something go for it to be healthier and happier. What's love got to do with it? Isn't it so obvious now?

Someone reminded me about the story of Ike, and Tina Turner in the movie called *What's Love Got to Do with It.*

That's why I titled this chapter "What's Love Got to Do with It." It is because it sort of sums this all up.

If you don't know the story, it's about love gone wrong. It's about control, desperation, and light. Ike Turner was a blues musician who meets an unknown at a bar and is drawn into her light. Her name is Tina. Turns out she is an incredible singer, and she's the light. She's the energy. A free spirit singer who's wonderful. He saw an opportunity and decided that she would be the thing that put his career over the top. The missing piece. She was unknown at this point and easily manipulated into believing that she was nothing without him. And he had total control over her.

It was quite the dance if you could view it from all angles. He was in fear of being just another nightclub act. She was in fear that she would never get her chance. And they fed each other's fear. And it became an addiction that was all-encompassing to both of them. The masculine controlling the feminine. And as always happens, even though the darkness was present, the light is always there.

At some point, Tina's light said, "You are more than this. This was a test. It's time to expand." And so she did. Although Ike was saying, "I'm going to dominate you, take all your money, and beat you into submission." She still had that quota of light, and she left. She jumped out of a moving car and ran for her light. Notice I didn't say life. She ran for her light. With nothing. She took nothing but her light. In the divorce, she only asked for her name, her light billboard. How the world identified her. No money. She had enough light in her to leave. She had enough light in her to fight back. What it took was her seeing what he was doing.

She could have left years earlier. But she didn't have an awareness of that yet. There were agreements, contracts, and bindings. There was history, need, and dependence. And still might have been if she hadn't acknowledged her own worth and awareness. Perhaps those distortions between them weren't complete.

Yet, at that point, Tina changed the game. She canceled the contracts, agreements and released the bindings. What, with light? She energetically cleared herself of the old story and then became Tina Turner. Her light quota grew and expanded, even through the trauma.

Perhaps it was the trauma that made the light expand? He didn't stop traumatizing her. She simply saw the whole picture. It wasn't love that caused him to need to control her. It was his fear. That control wasn't what it looked like. She would see him not as this scary controller. She could see through the illusion that she would be nothing without him. But the truth was the opposite. He needed her name. He needed to be able to say that he was why she was famous.

I'm not just talking about external. I'm talking about the fear in your body, the pain in your body, the control that's in your body. She freed herself energetically and made billions more as Tina Turner.

You may experience that now or as you shift. It will happen automatically. You have to be ready for your life to shift when you step onto this path of healing and enlightenment.

You'll notice that if you get caught in fear, moving through it happens faster now.

Fear is an emotional vibratory response to loss. As your vibration has increased, so has your ability to transmute those lower vibrations. Part of the shift is awareness. The shifting is directed by your higher intelligence. This knowing kicks in, and you have an awareness that says, "That's not true. I already know." And the fear has no place there anymore.

Some would say the fear becomes afraid of you. And anyone who's trying to control you is actually scared of you. Anything that's trying to control you, any government that's trying to control you, is horrified of you because the light is too bright.

That is what is at the root of most abusive relationships, you know. Fear. Most of the time, the abuser is afraid of the one they are abusing. Violence is their way of taking control of their own fear.

Your light is too bright now. You have accomplished all of this inner and outer work, and you are different, energetically. You are not the same. Things that appealed to you before won't appeal to you now. Many of my clients stopped smoking, left abusive relationships, or kicked addictions. It was easy after doing their work. Test it for yourself if you like.

A small warning. You have done all this work, and you want everyone else to feel like this. You want everyone else to be free. Regretfully, you can't change it for anyone but you. God Creator installed two little caveats. They are called the Law of Free Will and Sovereignty.

You can't pull everyone else off the ground. Release your need to change the story of that person. It is hard to witness others' destructions or failures. I know the feeling of "If you would just…" and they completely ignore you or call you crazy. Then you watch them fall again and again. We all have our agreements and contracts to experience. We all have to do this work.

Have you ever walked into a family gathering, and after 10 minutes, you are ready to go? Aunt Susan is criticizing everyone. Cousin Sally is pouting in the corner and throwing off pitiful vibes. Uncle Gerald is insisting that everyone listen to his stories, although you have heard them a million times. You have done all of this work to release the darkness and negative emotions. You have sacrificed money and time in courses and sessions. You have spent countless hours meditating and working on yourself only to subject yourself to this craziness a few times a year.

You are thinking, "What if all of my family would just take this one course, see this one person, or better yet, let me help them?" You may even be thinking, "I can fix them!" And, when you tell them what you have experienced and how it will benefit them, they look at you as though you have twelve heads.

You can't fix other people. What you can take comfort in is that we affect one another in different ways. As we do this work, yes, we affect others. We inspire others to do the work for themselves. Even though there may be 20 of your family there all playing off one another's triggers and wounded emotions, there might be one or two of them who are staring at you. Or secretly observing you the whole time of the gathering. Perhaps they will contact you after the gathering is over. Perhaps they will ask how to feel the way you do. There is your opening! Take it. Yet, recognize that until they reach out, there is nothing that you can do except be that light that they see, admire, and want for themselves. Good work!

Yes, we are all one. We all come from the same thought creation. We became single cells to have our own experiences. Then we go back to the light and compare and share the stories and experiences. It is a collective. So, as you remember your light, reclaim your authenticity, recalibrate your light quota, you affect those other parts of you automatically. They will see and feel that shift. It is, however, up to them to decide if they want to shift as well. You can create oneness through you. It is not through only resistance and being at the same frequency as the tyranny. It is through oneness we are also here to create a frequency of wholeness, and you're doing it.

Be the light. Just be that. You are not a rescuer. You are the light that shows everyone what else is possible. *Be* the light. That is the love. That is what love has to do with it.

So, let's have an experience. This is a way to heal relationships. It doesn't always have to be hard, though. You can always come back to this section when you are ready to face those relationships and heal them.

Pick someone who you are in resistance to or someone who you feel has been mean to you or mistreated you. You could, instead, pick someone whom you admire. We often think that others' lives are better than ours. That they have it easier than we do. Perhaps they have more money, fame, or love. Let's see how their lives are.

This is a great experience for getting a different perspective on life. Walking in someone else's shoes, so to speak. You can journal or record your experience for later review.

Let's go:

- Find a quiet place where you won't be disturbed.

- Take some deep, cleansing breaths. Focus on your breathing. Slow down your heartbeat. Release any anxiety or resistance by simply saying "release" as you exhale.

- Now, bring up the subject in your mind and memory. Bring up as much detail as possible so that you know you have made a good connection.

- What color is their hair, and how is it worn?

- What are they wearing in your image of them?

- What color are their eyes?

- Can you hear them? What does their voice sound like?

- How do they walk?

- What about their smell? Everyone has a distinct smell.

- How do you feel about them?

- If you could give them a compliment, what would it be?

- If you could make a request of them, what would it be?

- Think of the last time you saw them. What happened from your perspective?

- How did it end? In other words, how were things between you when you parted?

- Was there anything that wasn't said that you wish had been? Say it now.

- You might be surprised at how much detail you can get with those questions. Whatever you are feeling right now, just say "release." Any anxiety, envy, sadness, anger, or whatever the emotion, just say "release" because it is not even yours. Trust me on this one, and just play along.

- Now see yourself stepping into their form. Looking out of their eyes back at you. This is the good one. Ask the same questions from their perspective in looking at you. You can do it. Be objective. Don't try to judge the answers. Just record or journal them. Trust the impressions.

- What color is their hair, and how is it worn?

- What are they wearing in your image of them?

- What color are their eyes?

- Can you hear them? What does their voice sound like?

- How do they walk?

- What about their smell? Everyone has a distinct smell.

- How do you feel about them?

- If you could give them a compliment, what would it be?

- If you could make a request for them, what would it be?

- Think of the last time you saw them. What happened from your perspective?

- How did it end? In other words, how were things between you when you parted?

- Was there anything that wasn't said that you wish had been? Say it now.

How did you feel about that? How did it feel to look at you through their eyes? What were your observations? Were you surprised at some of them? I bet you were! I always am.

And the most important question is "how do you feel about them now"?

Chapter

Twenty-Three

The Lesson That Took Me
The Longest To Learn
By Dorothy Welty

Dorothy Welty

Dorothy Welty is a community college administrator and teacher. She holds an MS in psychology from Illinois State University. She is passionate about the power of education to change individual lives and the world in which we live. In her free time, Dorothy enjoys meditation, hiking, kayaking, writing, baking and a variety of other creative pursuits. You can reach Dorothy at dwelty50@gmail.com.

The Lesson That Took Me The Longest To Learn

By Dorothy Welty

On Oprah Winfrey's program, Super Soul Sunday, at the end of each conversation she has with her guests, she asks a series of questions, among which is, "What was the lesson that took you longest to learn?" What an excellent question! For me, the lesson that took me 57 years to learn was to always and every day listen to and follow my heart. Following one's heart is so vital because, as Maxime Lagace, an NHL goaltender from the Tampa Bay Lightning, said, "Your mind talks illusions. Your heart whispers the truth."

The truth of which the heart speaks is not the truth by the world's conditioning, judgments, and norms. It is the voice of the mind that will speak of those things. The voice of the heart tells us the truth of the yearnings of our soul. The heart's voice is the true self's efforts to break free and live in our authenticity. I came into the world, as I believe we all do, in touch with my heart. The degree to which we stay connected to our heart has a lot to do with whether the heart's voice is acknowledged, nurtured, and valued.

The environment I grew up in was faithful to the culture's conditioning, judgments, and norms. Appearances and stoicism were of the utmost importance. The voice of the mind was the dominant force. There was only one proper way to respond or behave no matter what the situation. The "proper" way was according to worldly standards created by family, culture, and community.

Attention to the heart was absent. Physical affection was absent. Even happiness, no matter how occasional, had to be tempered. Based on observation of the day-to-day reality of my childhood, the only common and acceptable emotional expression was anger. As a child, it was difficult to understand why my parents had so much anger at each other, their children, and others.

I now believe all emotions originate from an overall orientation of the individual to either love or fear. My home environment had a clear and robust orientation towards fear rather than love. The disposition around fear overpowered any opportunity to express love.

My father could say he loved us, but his only means of demonstrating his love was through money, giving you cash, or buying something for you with money. My mother only spoke of love as a reason for threatening or executing punishment. She told us she slapped or punished us because she loved us. To her, discipline was how you expressed love. The message my mother delivered was that earning one's worth through work and learning the "proper" thoughts and behavior was essential to avoiding her anger and punishment.

I was a timid, observant, obedient, but emotionally sensitive child raised by a very strict, demanding, and stoic mother. I feared my mother. I tried to be "good" and "proper" and not make waves in an angry and volatile household.

One particular day when I was about five or six years old, my mother was getting me ready for an outing. She called me into the master bedroom to fix my hair. She would pull back my bangs that would usually hang in my face with two little golden barrettes that had pretty pink roses on them. She knew I did not like the barrettes, and this particular day they were not in the corner of her dresser drawer where she kept them. She immediately and angrily shouted and accused me of taking the barrettes from her dresser. She demanded I admit what I had done with them and raised her hand, threatening to "whale the tar out of me." That day was the first time my mother threatened to hit me, and I began shaking and crying, making her angrier. After being slapped a couple of times, I still would not confess to a crime I had not committed. I had not taken the barrettes.

A couple of days later, when they surfaced in another part of her dresser drawer, she accused me of having moved them, which I had never done, and she punished me again by banishing me to my room. I remember the day she slapped me while I was shaking, crying, and pleading my innocence. A voice deep inside me told me I could never count on this woman to be on my side.

That incident changed who I was. I knew I was on my own. I could not count on my mother to have my back. My heart was breaking as I was shaking and crying, and that had only worsened my punishment. I knew I had to toughen up and lock away all the vulnerability of my heart. There was no place for the heart in this home.

I kept my feelings to myself and channeled the whispers of my heart into my interest in the arts. My artistic interests were not by way of anything in the environment. Though parents or teachers did not support these interests, I was self-motivated to pursue them independently. Paper, scissors, markers, and crayons were such a source of companionship through my childhood.

By high school, I desperately wanted to take woodshop, art, and theater classes. My mother would not allow it. To her woodshop, art and theater would not lead to productive employment. Instead, outside of the required high school curriculum, she would only approve me taking typing as she told me it would allow me to make a living as a secretary. I remember how angry I was at hearing that. I was her daughter, but she didn't know me.

I had started researching colleges the minute I started high school. I joined the high school debate team, which led to my plans to go to college and then law school. My father was supportive of my attending college. At that time, neither one of my older brothers had finished college, and I was his great hope for having a child graduate from college. He paid for my first year at Loyola University, after which my parents divorced. My mother had no interest in supporting my college education, and my father was despondent, having suffered a nervous breakdown. I was on my own. Before selling the home as part of the divorce, I moved home, got a job, bought a car, and got an apartment.

At the age of 25, the whispers of my heart led me to return to Loyola University, where I paid my way through college. My heart also led me to change my major from political science to psychology in a quest to make sense of my childhood. Independent since age 18, I had carried all the fear, anger, and resentment of my childhood with me. Not being able to find answers for all those destructive emotions, I continued my education in psychology and then made a career teaching psychology to others at colleges and universities.

My love of the arts and college came from my heart. After I was married, my heart desired a home. I wanted to raise my two boys in a house with a yard, not a rental apartment.

When my oldest son became school age, we were still living in university family housing. I was about to finish graduate school, and I wanted our family to have a home. Between my husband and me, we had three part-time jobs that put us just above the poverty line and would not qualify us for a mortgage. I was undaunted. I found a home for sale that was the only one we could afford. It was a 750 square foot house built in 1877 that looked like it was on the brink of being condemned. The limestone foundation was crumbling, and the termite damage was extensive. After being turned down three times, it took weeks and several attempts to secure a mortgage, but we finally got the little shack to call our own. With my husband and I being very handy, we turned it into a cozy little cottage. Five years later, I was pregnant with my second son, and there was no way another child would fit into the 750 square foot house.

Ever since we had moved to the central Illinois college town, I had dreamt of living on one of the two historic, tree-lined streets on either side of the university. As I drove down one of them one day on my way to somewhere, one of the homes I had most admired, a 1920s American four square, that needed some tender loving care was for sale and having an open house.

It was a hot, humid summer day in August. I pulled over immediately and got out to take a look. There had only been one owner of the home who was now a widow. She had raised her children there, but she now had very advanced Alzheimer's disease. Her grown children had moved her to assisted living and were selling the house.

To say the house didn't show well was an understatement. The kitchen looked like the 1970s. The rest of the house looked like it had not been touched since 1920. But, the bones of the house were good. I felt the home was way overpriced, not for the neighborhood, but for all the work someone would have to put into it.

I grabbed the flyer that had a picture of this beautiful American four square. I went home, cut out the photo, and taped it to my computer monitor on my desk at work. From the moment I set foot in that home, my heart longed to live there. I could see our family living there. Each day I stared at that picture as my heart whispered its love for that home. I just couldn't let go of seeing our family living in that house celebrating the New Year.

I brought my husband to see the house, and I knew that it spoke to his heart, but his mind saw the price, and he let go instantly of any thoughts we could ever buy that house. I declared to my husband that this would be our next home. He thought I was crazy.

I kept tabs on that listing as it sat on the market. The price had come down a bit by October but was still out of reach for our budget. I convinced my husband that we should put in a low bid we could afford. We put in the offer. It was rejected immediately without so much as a counteroffer. A few weeks later, the realtor notified me that there was another offer on the house. She was trying to encourage us to bid again. I said we couldn't bid more than we previously did. I told her I felt the house was still overpriced for all the work it needed.

The owner's adult children accepted the offer made by the other party, but interestingly it fell through a couple of weeks later. I had never wavered and still looked at the picture of that house taped to my computer monitor and saw that home as ours. I told my husband the week after Thanksgiving, but just before the Christmas holidays, I wanted us to put in another bid, just $5,000 more than our previous low bid. He thought I was crazy but knew he needed to humor me. As Thanksgiving approached, the snow and cold came. I had put my mind in service of my heart and calculated that the owners would be more open to our offer as heating bills for an empty house racked up. I was right. They accepted our offer with the stipulation of a 30-day closing. We celebrated the New Year in our new home. We upgraded the wiring, stripped the carpet, refinished the beautiful wood floors, painted the entire house inside and out ourselves, and planted beautiful gardens. We lived there for five years. That was the happiest five years of my life to that point.

By far, the best choices I made in life came from listening to the whispers of my heart. The choices made that were of the mind did not turn out so well. It would take 22 years in an unhappy marriage and seven more years of lessons after my divorce before I became miserable enough to quiet the illusions of the mind and open up to honor the whispers of my heart every day of my life.

As I left my marriage behind and reflected on life to that point, I realized the mind that lived by fear dictated most of my choices. Though I had loved my husband, fear of not doing the "right" thing when I became pregnant drove my decision to marry. My decision to stay in an unhappy marriage was a decision of the mind, caused by illusions of fear and doubt that kept me bound to my unhappiness. The truth of my heart had whispered to me for so long, and I had not listened. The heart's voice grew louder until it could not be ignored or stifled.

When I finally honored the voice of my heart and found the faith and courage to leave the marriage, I thought all would be well. I just needed to break away from an unfulfilling marriage. However, my mind that had been well trained and conditioned was still the ruler.

I would endure a lot more suffering before realizing that I had to live each day from my heart. My mind needed to be used to serve my heart rather than override my heart. I did not thoroughly learn that lesson until I was 57.

As I followed my heart and moved to Colorado to live in 300 days of sunshine each year with a view of the mountains, I made a personal commitment to have my heart rule every moment of every day. I committed to using my mind to serve my heart, and I am a kinder, gentler, and softer person. I have made it full circle back to the tender heart I had as a child. At every choice point in each day, I am continuously checking in with the whispers of my heart. I am finally at peace.

Made in the USA
Middletown, DE
20 January 2022

59208943R00176